Pro Freeware and Open Source Solutions for Business

Money-Saving Options for Small Enterprises

Second Edition

Phillip Whitt

Apress®

Pro Freeware and Open Source Solutions for Business: Money-Saving Options for Small Enterprises

Phillip Whitt
Columbus, GA, USA

ISBN-13 (pbk): 978-1-4842-8840-5   ISBN-13 (electronic): 978-1-4842-8841-2
https://doi.org/10.1007/978-1-4842-8841-2

Managing Director, Apress Media LLC: Welmoed Spahr
Acquisitions Editor: Divya Modi
Development Editor: James Markham
Coordinating Editor: Divya Modi

Cover designed by eStudioCalamar

Cover image designed by Freepik (www.freepik.com)

Distributed to the book trade worldwide by Springer Science+Business Media New York, 1 New York Plaza, Suite 4600, New York, NY 10004-1562, USA. Phone 1-800-SPRINGER, fax (201) 348-4505, e-mail orders-ny@ springer-sbm.com, or visit www.springeronline.com. Apress Media, LLC is a California LLC and the sole member (owner) is Springer Science + Business Media Finance Inc (SSBM Finance Inc). SSBM Finance Inc is a **Delaware** corporation.

For information on translations, please e-mail booktranslations@springernature.com; for reprint, paperback, or audio rights, please e-mail bookpermissions@springernature.com.

Apress titles may be purchased in bulk for academic, corporate, or promotional use. eBook versions and licenses are also available for most titles. For more information, reference our Print and eBook Bulk Sales web page at http://www.apress.com/bulk-sales.

Any source code or other supplementary material referenced by the author in this book is available to readers on GitHub via the book's product page, located at www.apress.com/. For more detailed information, please visit http://www.apress.com/source-code.

Printed on acid-free paper

This book is dedicated to my wonderful family. Their support and patience while I was writing this book over the past several months will forever be appreciated.

Table of Contents

About the Author

Phillip Whitt is an author and small business owner. His professional experience spans more than three decades. Many of those years were spent in marketing and advertising managerial roles in the retail building materials business. Since 2000, Phillip has owned and operated a film-to-video and image editing/design business. Over the years, he's learned that budgeting is an important factor that helps contribute to the bottom line of any business.

Phillip is the author of *Beginning Photo Retouching and Restoration Using GIMP* (Apress Publishing, 2014). He is trained and certified in the use of a number of open source software programs such as OpenOffice, GIMP, Inkscape, Scribus, and Ubuntu Linux.

About the Technical Reviewer

Massimo Nardone holds a Master of Science degree in Computing Science from the University of Salerno, Italy. He worked as a PCI QSA and senior lead IT security/cloud/SCADA architect for many years and currently works as security, cloud, and SCADA lead IT architect for Hewlett Packard, Finland. He has more than 20 years of work experience in IT including security, SCADA, cloud computing, IT infrastructure, mobile, security, and WWW technology areas for both national and international projects. Massimo has worked as a project manager, cloud/SCADA lead IT architect, software engineer, research engineer, chief security architect, and software specialist. He worked as visiting lecturer and supervisor for exercises at the Networking Laboratory of the Helsinki University of Technology (Aalto University). He has been programming and teaching how to program with Perl, PHP, Java, VB, Python, C/C++, and MySQL for more than 20 years. He is the author of *Pro Android Games* (Apress, 2015). He holds four international patents (PKI, SIP, SAML, and Proxy areas).

Acknowledgments

I would like to thank the team at Apress, especially Louise Corrigan, Divya Modi, and James Markham. Their patience, professionalism, and guidance are greatly appreciated.

I also owe a great deal of gratitude to Mark Lupo and Todd Carlisle of the Columbus, GA SBDC (Small Business Development Center) office. Their years of experience in assisting the development and growth of small businesses give them a valuable perspective; they know very well that any business can always benefit by cutting costs when feasible. They also know how important it is for new business upstarts to save as much as possible. Their counsel during the development of this book was invaluable and is greatly appreciated.

Introduction

I first encountered a free, open source program called GIMP (GNU Image Manipulation Program) which is a free alternative to Adobe Photoshop back in the early 2000s. At the time, I was a die-hard fan of Photoshop and dismissed any further exploration of GIMP after a few minutes. In those days, when I needed software for my business, I just drove to the nearest office supply store and purchased what I wanted. Back then I thought paid, proprietary software was the only viable option (and over time, I ended up paying a small fortune for software). My views on open source and free software changed drastically a few short years later.

In early 2009, I was launching my small business in a new city that my wife and I had been planning to relocate to for a couple of years. It just so happened that our move coincided with the Great Recession that had been unfolding in 2008. The company that employed my wife set her up with a computer and separate high-speed Internet line to work remotely, only to (along with many others) lay her off about a month later.

Like many other families, the financial crisis impacted us in a negative way. Our relationship with money was forever changed, and careful budgeting became a top priority.

My wife decided it was time to update her resume in order to search for a job that would allow her to work remotely for health reasons. We purchased a resume software program for about $20.00 and a new, discontinued model computer at a deep discount. The computer (which was running Windows Vista) did not come with Microsoft Word installed, which was necessary (or so I thought) for using the resume creation software.

At that time, the retail package for MS Word cost about $100, which was more than our budget allowed. I recalled trying out the free program GIMP several years earlier and wondered if there was a free alternative to MS Word. I quickly discovered there indeed was a program called OpenOffice (now Apache OpenOffice) that is a free, fully functioning alternative to MS Word and compatible with Word files.

After downloading and trying it out, I was very pleasantly surprised. It worked with the resume creation software just fine, and my search for a document creation program ended right there. And the best part was the license allowed me to copy it, share it, and install it on multiple computers—all at no cost!

My discovery of OpenOffice was almost as good as finding a 100 dollar bill I had forgotten about. With our situation the way it was, it was truly a fortunate find; my wife could work on her resume, and I could install OpenOffice on my computer and create marketing materials to acquire new customers.

Note Although Apache OpenOffice is still available, Chapter 1 of this book covers LibreOffice, which was forked from OpenOffice in 2010. The two programs are essentially the same, except LibreOffice is updated more often and has ostensibly become one of the leading alternatives to Microsoft Office over the years.

Who This Book Is For

This book was written primarily with business owners and managers in mind, but any frugal-minded computer user can find it useful. For the business owner who carefully watches over the expenses of their enterprise, this book points the way to some viable, free software solutions. It can be especially helpful to new, small business upstarts, serving as a reference to help quickly find viable alternatives to expensive software.

Operating capital is often limited during the early phase of launching a new venture, so (along with other commonsense budgeting strategies) it pays to keep as much cash in your business as possible (Figure 1). Using free software when possible can help you accomplish this.

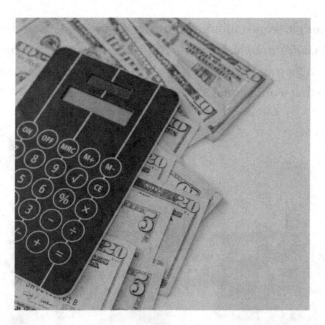

Figure 1. *Using freeware and open source software can help you keep more cash in your business (Photo: Karolina Grabowska/Pexels)*

There are many free software titles available that you may not be aware exist. When I wrote the first edition of this book, I took a poll of about 50 business owners asking certain questions about open source software. Although it wasn't a large number of people, I thought the answers were telling. Only two of those polled knew about open source programs such as GIMP and OpenOffice—most of them didn't realize there's a large assortment of free software options available that could potentially save them money.

Potential savings will vary depending on the nature of the business and its software requirements. Savings can amount to several hundred dollars annually for freelance graphic designers to thousands of dollars for larger organizations.

Schools, teachers, and students can benefit as well. For example, if a high school operating under tight budget restraints can't afford the Adobe Creative Cloud suite of products for a digital art class, there are a number of free alternatives available.

Open source graphics programs such as GIMP and Inkscape are free to install and use on multiple computers, and the good part is students can install them on their own home computer(s), saving the household budget some money.

A class with multiple workstations as shown in Figure 2—let's say ten, for example—could save about $3,600 annually, based on Adobe's educational pricing of $14.99 (for each app) per month for a single user. (Photoshop and Illustrator are currently $14.99 each per month, so that would equal $29.98 per user each month.)

Figure 2. *Using open source software instead of the Adobe CC can save about $1200 annually on ten workstations (Photo source: Pixabay)*

What's the Difference Between Freeware and Open Source Software?

As the question implies, freeware and open source software are not quite the same. Although each type may be used free of charge, the differences lie mainly in the terms of use set forth by the licensing agreement. For the purposes of this book, free means that all of the programs outlined can be used free of charge, both for personal and commercial purposes.

However, free as defined by the *Free Software Foundation* and the *Open Source Initiative* means freedom, as in the freedom to modify the source code, make copies for others, and install on multiple computers, to name a few examples. In essence, the user is free from the restrictions imposed by the license of paid proprietary software.

Freeware

Generally speaking, freeware is proprietary software that can be used free of charge, but the creator retains all of the rights to the code, so modifying it is not permitted. The terms of use regarding freeware can vary depending on the creator. Some freeware titles are created by individual developers, while others are created by corporations. One freeware program's license might allow you to make and distribute free copies to friends and coworkers but prohibit selling them. Another might only allow you to make one backup copy and prohibit any type of distribution. *It's always advisable to read the license agreement carefully before installing and using freeware.*

Some freeware programs have limited features with the option to upgrade to a more feature-rich, paid version of the program. Some of the ones described in this book fall under that category—the free versions are basic and may be perfectly fine for business upstarts or small enterprises with only a few people (or the solo entrepreneur).

Some freeware is web-based, so there is nothing to download because it operates in your browser. You don't have to worry about upgrades (although some of them offer an option to upgrade to a premium paid version).

One example is Pixlr (which is covered in Chapter 4). Pixlr is a web-based program for editing photos and creating designs. You'll need to upgrade to the premium versions to unlock all the features, but you still have access to most of the features. For basic use, the free version of Pixlr should work fine for most users.

Open Source Software

Open source refers to software that usually falls under some version of the *GPL* (General Public License). Open source means that the software code is made available so that developers can modify or improve the software. Also, in addition to being free of charge, you can make and distribute copies and install it on multiple computers (Figure 3).

Figure 3. *Free and open source software under the terms of the GPL can be freely copied and distributed (Photo: Karolina Grabowska/Pexels)*

Note There may be some open source software out there that's not necessarily available at no cost. However, the open source programs outlined in this book are; to learn more about open source licenses, visit `https://opensource.org/licenses`.

Examples of Businesses and Organizations That Use Free and Open Source Software

Starter Story (`www.starterstory.com`) is an online resource for startup businesses that provides business ideas, growth ideas, inspirational stories, and more. Here are links to two case studies by Pat Walls of business enterprises that use the open source programs LibreOffice and GIMP:

- This one highlights nine companies that use LibreOffice for their productivity—`www.starterstory.com/tools/libreoffice/companies-using`.

- This one highlights 27 companies that use GIMP (a free Photoshop alternative) for their image editing and graphics creation needs—`https://starterstory.com/tools/gimp/companies-using`.

One important point to keep in mind is that migrating from proprietary to open source software (especially on a large scale) must be done properly. It takes time to get everyone involved acclimated, and it is generally done gradually. In short, there must be a plan in place. Switching from Microsoft Office to LibreOffice on 100 workstations all at once could be very disruptive to the organization.

There is a helpful article for organizations on properly migrating from proprietary to free/open source software published by TechRepublic (Jack Wallen, September 1, 2014)—www.techrepublic.com/article/5-tips-on-migrating-to-open-source-software/.

It might not be possible to completely escape the necessity of using proprietary software on at least some workstations. As an example, a company might determine that proprietary software could be reduced to a few workstations. Open source software can be installed on the remaining workstations (Figure 4).

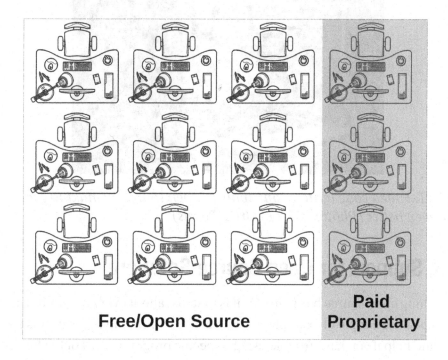

Figure 4. *By using proprietary software on a minimum number of workstations, open source software can be used on the remaining ones*

Supporting Open Source Software (and Freeware)

Open source software (and for that matter, some freeware that is developed by individuals) is available at no charge, but donations are important for continued development. Many of the people involved in the development of open source software work on a voluntary basis.

Open source can be supported in other ways as well: becoming an advocate, giving away copies, teaching others how to use specific open source programs, writing about open source, etc.

People talented in writing code can contribute by making their favorite programs even better (Figure 5).

Figure 5. *Talented code writers contribute to open source by making good software even better (Photo: Ricardo Ortiz/Pexels)*

Getting Support for Open Source Software

One great thing open source has going for it is that just about every program (GIMP and Inkscape are a couple of examples) has an active community. The forums are great places to find help if you have trouble using a specific program. Most of the forum members are glad to help out. It may even be easier to get help for open source programs than their proprietary counterparts. Calling technical support and being on hold for long periods, paying for support that may not always provide the correct solution, and other hassles are common with proprietary software.

Some open source programs offer paid technical support, particularly if the software is designed for larger enterprises. However, there are often avenues of free support available in user forums and downloadable documentation.

YouTube is another valuable learning resource. This video platform now hosts just about any kind of tutorial you can imagine. More often than not, you'll be able to find good tutorials on any given software title.

Note LinkedIn (`www.linkedin.com`) is another way to connect with open source users. There are groups for many (if not most) of the software programs examined in this book. Group members are very helpful, and your questions will usually be answered quickly.

Summary

Hopefully, you are enthused about the potential savings offered by freeware and open source software. Here's what we covered in this Introduction:

- Who This Book Is For

- What's the Difference Between Freeware and Open Source Software?

- Examples of Businesses and Organizations That Use Free and Open Source Software

- Supporting Open Source Software (and Freeware)

- Getting Support for Open Source Software

Now, feel free to look around in this book for the software solutions you need. There are additional software titles mentioned in Appendix B of this book.

CHAPTER 1

Office Productivity, Note-Taking, Accounting, and PDF Creation

Everyone in the civilized world has heard of software programs like Microsoft Word, QuickBooks, etc. Although the alternative software titles we'll look at shortly have been around for years and are no secret, I'd venture to guess that there are many business owners who have never heard of them (or at least not all of them).

This chapter looks at free software alternatives to commercial programs commonly used in office environments. This software is used for creating letters and documents, creating PDF files, and handling business accounting.

Here's a quick look at the software titles covered in this chapter:

- **LibreOffice**: A full-featured office productivity suite for creating documents, spreadsheets, etc.

- **FreeOffice**: A free alternative to Microsoft Office for personal or small business use

- **Simplenote**: A free, open source note-taking application you can share and sync across devices

- **Zim**: An open source note-taking application for single users

- **GnuCash**: A powerful open source accounting program

- **Manager**: An easy-to-use, free accounting program with upgrade options

- **PDF reDirect**: A handy PDF creation tool with upgrade options

1

© Phillip Whitt 2022
P. Whitt, *Pro Freeware and Open Source Solutions for Business*, https://doi.org/10.1007/978-1-4842-8841-2_1

All of the programs discussed in this chapter work in the Windows environment, and most work in macOS and Linux as well. The first two programs we'll look at are alternatives to Microsoft Word and Office.

LibreOffice: The Powerful Free Office Suite

Large organizations have embraced this open source software package over the past several years for good reason: it suits their needs and saves them a lot of money.

Here are a few facts about LibreOffice at a glance:

- **Alternative to**: Microsoft365 Apps for Business

- **Website**: www.libreoffice.org

- **License**: MPL V2 (Mozilla Public License)

- **Current Version**: 7.3.4.2

- **Operating Systems**: Windows, macOS, Linux

- **Potential Savings**: $8.25 per month (per user)

LibreOffice is the open source powerhouse office suite made available by the Document Foundation, which is a self-regulating body dedicated to this program's ongoing development. It's comprised of former leading members who were involved in the development of the familiar office suite OpenOffice (www.openoffice.org) but forked it into the now well-established LibreOffice.

Because LibreOffice is free and open source, it can be installed on as many computers as needed in your organization (Figure 1-1).

Figure 1-1. *LibreOffice can be installed on as many computers as necessary in your business*

Note   This full-featured suite can create just about any kind of business document, spreadsheet, chart, or database you need. I use LibreOffice Writer on a regular basis for my writing and document creation needs. LibreOffice is highly compatible with Microsoft Office.

LibreOffice Modules

The LibreOffice suite contains the following programs:

- *Writer*: A word processing program similar to Microsoft Word.

- *Calc*: Calc is a spreadsheet program similar to Microsoft Excel.

- *Impress*: This is a multimedia presentation program similar to Microsoft PowerPoint.

- *Base*: A database program similar to Microsoft Access.

- *Draw*: Draw lets you add visual impact to your documents by creating anything from simple graphics to detailed, technical drawings.

Writer

Writer is more or less the equivalent to Microsoft Word. It is an extremely capable application that can create a wide array of documents. It can be used to create business letters, resumes, newsletters, marketing pieces, etc.

Figure 1-2 shows a screenshot of an actual document created in LibreOffice to distribute to newly hired stock crew members for a local grocery store (the simple graphics on the front page were created in the Draw module).

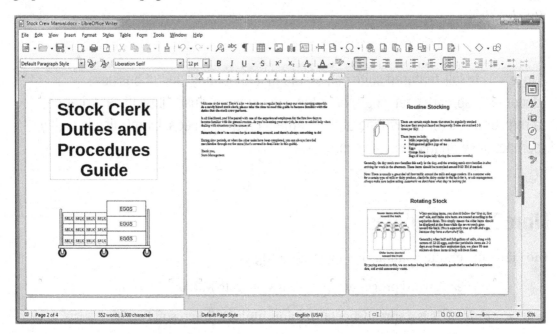

Figure 1-2. *This document for newly hired stock crew workers was created for a local grocery store using LibreOffice*

It can be used for creating address labels, business cards, business letters, and other business documents. LibreOffice's functionality can be increased by utilizing additional templates available to download for creating brochures, accounting charts, etc. They are available to download at no cost from https://extensions.libreoffice.org/.

The small business magazine article as shown in this screenshot (Figure 1-3) was written using LibreOffice without the aid of additional templates, so it's easy to imagine the possibility of what you can create by utilizing the templates and extensions that are available for this powerful application.

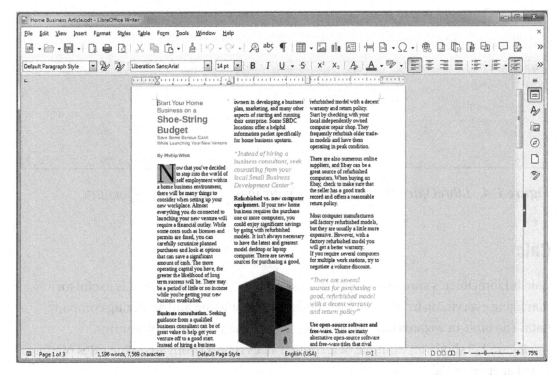

Figure 1-3. *A magazine article created using LibreOffice*

LibreOffice saves documents in its native ODF (.odt) format by default; it also allows you to save your document in a wide variety of formats, including several Microsoft Word formats (Figure 1-4). The document can also be exported as a PDF.

ODF Text Document
ODF Text Document Template
Flat XML ODF Text Document
Unified Office Format text
Word 2007–365
Word 2007–365 Template
Word 2003 XML
Word 97–2003
Word 97–2003 Template
DocBook
HTML Document (Writer)
Rich Text
Text
Text - Choose Encoding
Office Open XML Text (Transitional)
Word 2007–365 VBA

Word 2007–365

☑ Automatic file name extension
☐ Save with password
☐ Encrypt with GPG key
☐ Edit filter settings

Save   Cancel

Figure 1-4. *LibreOffice Writer can save your work in a variety of formats*

Calc

Calc is LibreOffice's spreadsheet program similar to Microsoft Excel. It is useful for managing everything from household budgets to managing and analyzing company data. The built-in wizards help new users navigate the wide array of features.

Figure 1-5 shows an example of an online sales report (from an online sales platform I use) opened in Calc.

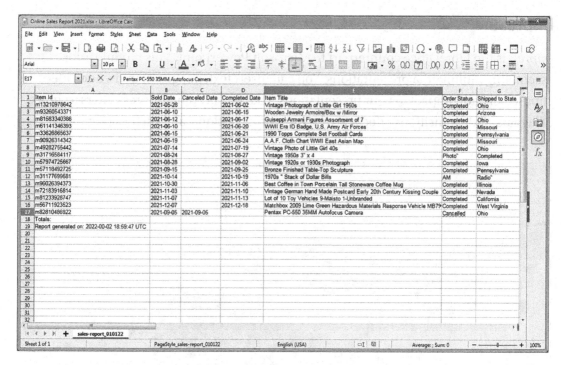

Figure 1-5. *A sales report opened in Calc*

Calc's default format is ODF Spreadsheet (.ods) but will save your work in various formats, including Excel 2007-365 (.xlxs) as shown in Figure 1-6.

ODF Spreadsheet
ODF Spreadsheet Template
Flat XML ODF Spreadsheet
Unified Office Format spreadsheet
Excel 2007–365
Excel 2007–365 Template
Excel 97–2003
Excel 97–2003 Template
Data Interchange Format
dBASE
HTML Document (Calc)
SYLK
Text CSV
Office Open XML Spreadsheet
Excel 2007–365 (macro-enabled)

Excel 2007–365

☑ Automatic file name
   extension
☐ Save with password
☐ Encrypt with GPG key
☐ Edit filter settings

                                                        Save   Cancel

Figure 1-6. *Calc can save your spreadsheet in a number of different formats, including Excel 2007-365*

Impress

Impress is the LibreOffice counterpart to Microsoft PowerPoint. This module is for assembling multimedia presentations. You can insert text, images, sounds, and video clips to help add impact to your presentations. Like PowerPoint, Impress offers a choice of layouts, slide transitions effects, styles, formatting options, and themes (Figure 1-7).

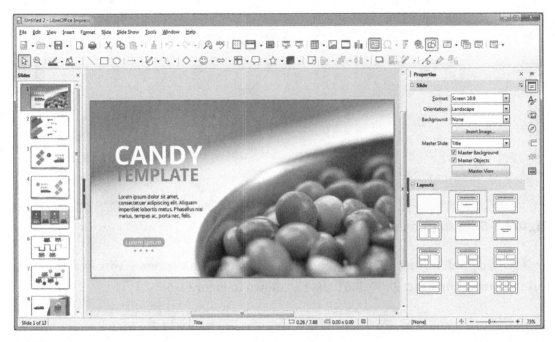

Figure 1-7. *Impress can create multimedia presentations similar to PowerPoint*

Base

Base is the full-featured front-end database module of LibreOffice. It integrates with the other LibreOffice applications. It can be used for creating tables, queries, forms, and reports. When first launched, a wizard opens to help you get your database up and running (Figure 1-8).

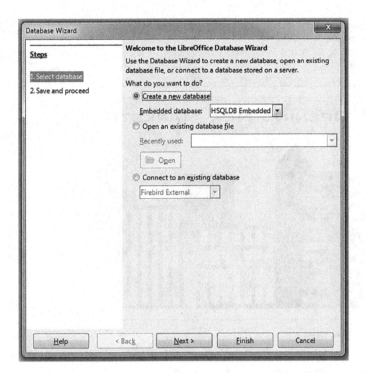

Figure 1-8. *Base provides a wizard to help new users get started*

Draw

This module lets you create and add graphical elements to your documents, create flowcharts, and create technical sketches. Draw offers a number of options for shapes, free-form drawing, gradients and fill colors, callouts, etc. It's easy to use and helpful for creating graphics to add visual impact to your documents (Figure 1-9).

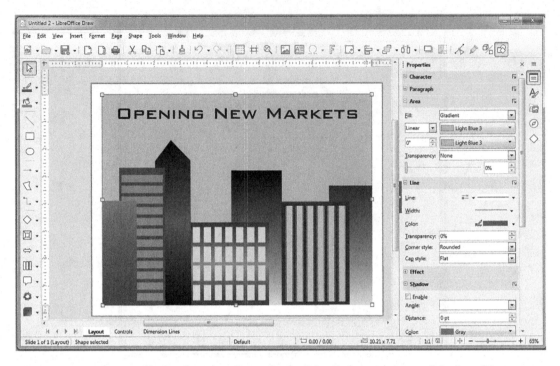

Figure 1-9. *Draw allows the creation of graphical elements to add visual impact to your documents. (Illustration by Phillip Whitt)*

LibreOffice Support

LibreOffice is now one of the leading free, open source office productivity suites. If you need help with some aspect of LibreOffice, one of the best places to look for assistance is on the *Get Help* page of the LibreOffice.org website. There are also numerous YouTube tutorials that are very helpful.

Although the Document Foundation does not offer professional support services, there is a certification system in place for those various professionals who deliver and sell services around LibreOffice. To learn more, visit `www.libreoffice.org/get-help/professional-support/`.

FreeOffice 2021: A Free Alternative to Microsoft Office for Personal and Business Use

FreeOffice is a free office productivity suite from the German company SoftMaker. Compatible with Microsoft office, it's essentially a slimmed down version of SoftMaker Office, which offers packages for home and larger-scale enterprises.

- **Alternative to**: Microsoft 365 Apps for Business

- **Website**: www.freeoffice.com/en/

- **License**: Proprietary

- **Current Version**: 2021

- **Operating Systems**: Windows, macOS, Linux

- **Potential Savings**: $8.25 per month (per user)

FreeOffice does limit installation to one (1) computer belonging to an organization, so it's ideal for the small company with just one to five people (Figure 1-10). The license also states you can "Make a reasonable number of backup copies for archive purposes, as long as the backup copies are not distributed."

Figure 1-10. *The FreeOffice terms of use limit installation to one (1) computer in a business organization*

To read the license, follow this link: www.freeoffice.com/en/download/applications; then click the *License Agreement (EULA)* button.

FreeOffice Apps

The FreeOffice 2021 suite offers three applications:

- *TextMaker:* A word processing program similar to Microsoft Word

- *PlanMaker:* A spreadsheet program similar to Microsoft Excel

- *Presentations:* A multimedia presentation program similar to Microsoft PowerPoint

TextMaker

TextMaker is similar to Microsoft Word. Like LibreOffice, it's a capable application that can create a wide array of documents. It can be used to create just about any kind of document Word or LibreOffice can.

After FreeOffice has been downloaded and installed, a window requesting a product key will appear; just enter your email address in the field shown and it will be sent to you.

After entering the product key, a window displaying options for the interface theme is displayed. You can select *Ribbon* or one of the *Classic* modes. The Ribbon mode is selected by default, as shown in Figure 1-11.

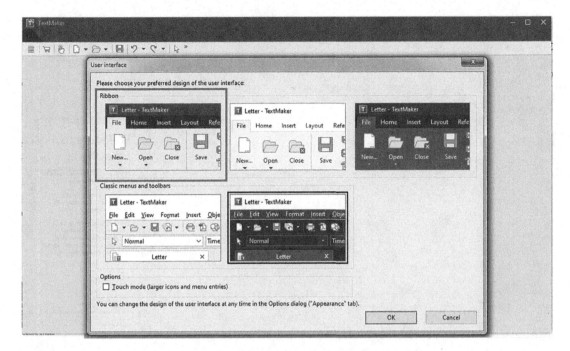

Figure 1-11. *FreeOffice TextMaker offers several options for using the Ribbon or Classic modes*

After TextMaker has been launched, the *Sidebar* to the right of the window offers tips and tricks for using the program (Figure 1-12).

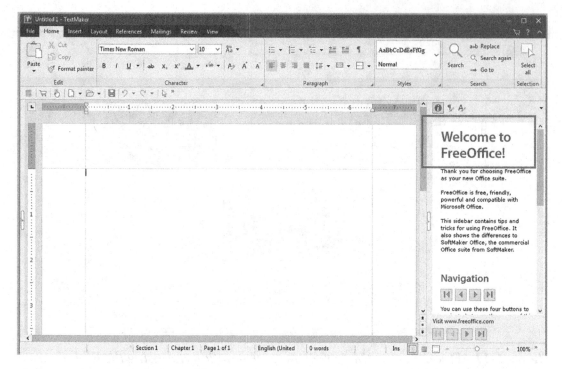

Figure 1-12. *The Sidebar offers tips and tricks for using FreeOffice TextMaker*

TextMaker offers the core functionality one would expect from a word processor. You can write business letters, resumes, marketing letters—just about any type of business document you need. By accessing the *AutoShape* or *Lines* menu, basic graphics can be created to add impact to your documents (Figure 1-13).

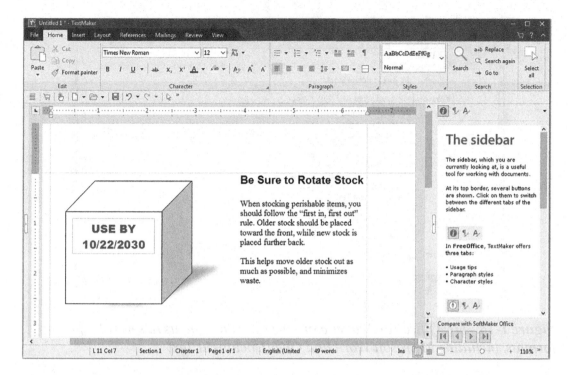

Figure 1-13. *Basic graphics can be created to add visual impact to your documents*

As Figure 1-14 shows, TextMaker documents can be saved in its native TextMaker format, as well as several others, including Microsoft Word and OpenDocument Text (.odt). The document can also be exported as a PDF.

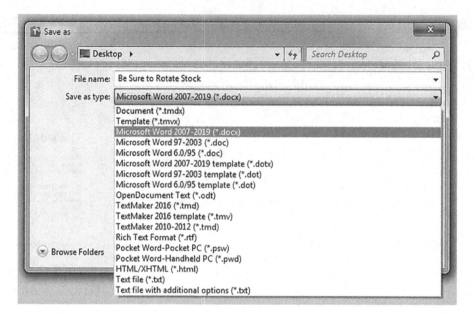

Figure 1-14. *FreeOffice TextMaker can save your documents in several different formats, including Microsoft Word and OpenDocument Text*

PlanMaker

FreeOffice PlanMaker is similar to Microsoft Excel or LibreOffice Calc, used for creating and working with spreadsheets. It offers over 430 calculation functions. FreeOffice PlanMaker can be used for working with mathematics, statistics, financial information, and data analysis.

Figure 1-15 shows the sales report that was originally generated as a CSV file and then opened in PlanMaker.

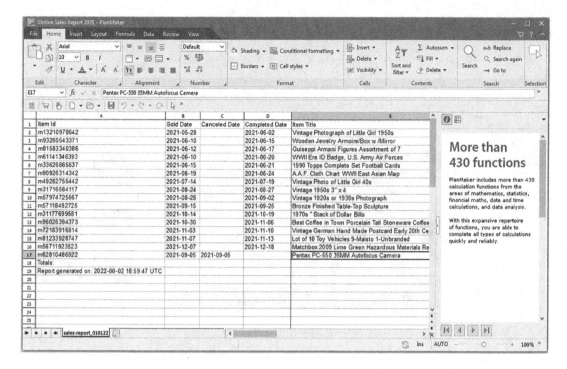

Figure 1-15. *A sales report opened in FreeOffice PlanMaker*

Your spreadsheets can be saved in several different formats, including the native PlanMaker (.pmdx) or Microsoft Excel. It can also be exported as a PDF.

Presentations

FreeOffice Presentations is similar to Microsoft PowerPoint, which is used to create presentations. It offers numerous functions for presentation design: insert photos and drawings, movie and sound clips, and text frames.

You can include animations and slide transitions (using OpenGL graphics acceleration) to create presentations with impact.

Presentations offers a basic set of slide designs (Figure 1-16).

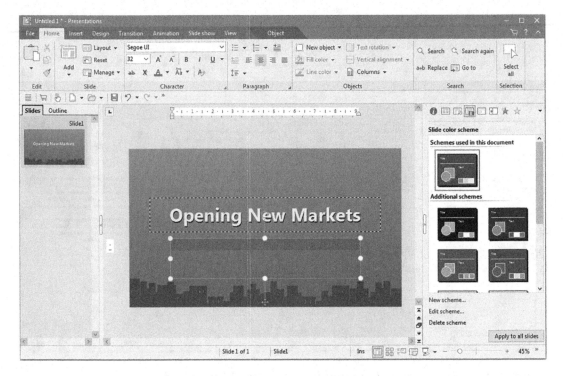

Figure 1-16. *FreeOffice offers a basic set of designs*

FreeOffice Support

One of the best places to seek support for FreeOffice is from the *Help* menu (Figure 1-17). From here, you'll have access to the Help dialog, user manual, and the SoftMaker website.

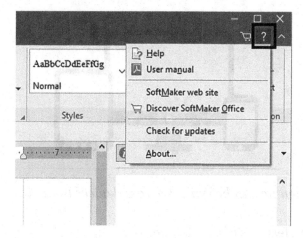

Figure 1-17. *The FreeOffice Help menu*

Simplenote: A Free Note-Taking Application for Syncing Across Devices

Simplenote is a free, lightweight note-taking application. It can be used on iOS, Android, Mac, Windows, and Linux.

- **Alternative to**: Evernote

- **Website**: https://simplenote.com/

- **License**: (GPL-2.0) General Public License

- **Operating Systems**: iOS, Android, Windows, macOS, Linux

- **Potential Savings**: $7.99-$14.99 per month

Your notes can be synced across your devices (Figure 1-18), making collaboration with other team members easy.

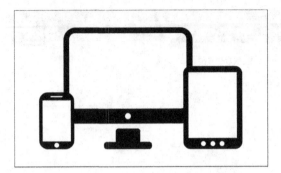

Figure 1-18. *Simplenote can be synced across devices to make collaboration easy*

Here are the main features of Simplenote:

- Notes automatically stay updated across devices; no "sync" button to press.

- Notes are automatically backed up.

- Add tags to notes to make searching for them fast.

- Write, preview, and publish your notes in the Markdown format.

- Collaborate; share a to-do list, post instructions to team members, etc.

- It's totally free to use.

The first step is to click the *Sign Up* button from the Simplenote home page. Once you're signed up, you can start using the program. With Simplenote, you can preview your notes, insert a checklist, access the *Info* window (such as when a note was last created or synced), or access the *Actions* menu. Figure 1-19 shows a sample of an actual note I created during the updating phase of this book.

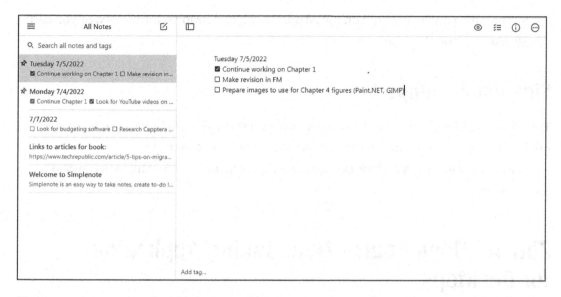

Figure 1-19. *A sample of notes I took for use in the updating phase of this book*

Simplenote is a great tool for sharing a to-do list with instructions for multiple employees with a Simplenote account. Just add each one's email address in the *Collaborate* submenu (Figure 1-20). Each recipient will be notified by email that a note created in Simplenote has been shared with them.

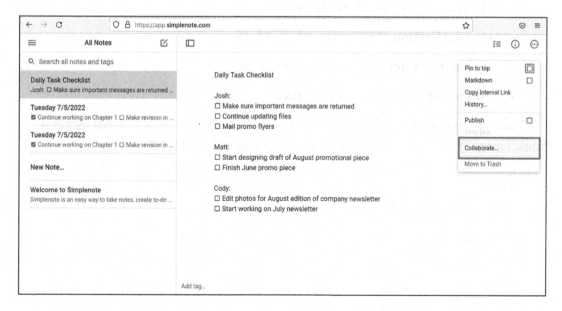

Figure 1-20. *To-do lists, instructions, or other notes can be shared with other Simplenote users for collaboration*

Simplenote can be installed on iOS, Android, Mac, Windows, and Linux, or you can simply use it in your browser.

Simplenote Support

The *Help Center* page addresses just about any question you might have (or issue you might encounter) with Simplenote: `https://simplenote.com/help/`.

There are also several videos on YouTube that provide reviews and overviews of Simplenote.

Zim: An Open Source Note-Taking Application for Desktops

Zim is an application for taking notes, creating journals and to-do lists, as well as inserting images and links to websites, images, or documents in the form of wiki pages.

- **Alternative to**: Notion

- **Website**: `www.zim-wiki.org`

- **License**: GNU General Public License

- **Current Version**: 0.69.1

- **Operating Systems**: Windows, macOS, Linux

- **Potential Savings**: $48.00 annually

Zim is an open source software offered under the terms of the GPL (GNU General Public License) and can be installed on multiple computers (Figure 1-21).

Figure 1-21. *Zim can be installed on as many computers as necessary in your business*

Zim is a useful organizational tool (something like a digital planner/notebook). Here are some of the program's uses (as described on the Zim wiki page):

- Keep an archive of notes.

- Keep a daily or weekly journal.

- Take notes during meetings or lectures.

- Organize task lists.

- Draft blog entries and emails.

- Do brainstorming.

Even though Zim is open source and can be installed on multiple computers, it's primarily designed for single users. You can insert links and attach external files such as images (Figure 1-22).

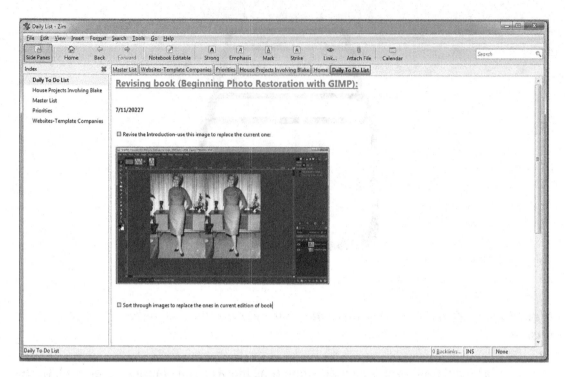

Figure 1-22. *Links to URLs, other Zim pages, and images can be added to you notes*

Note   Zim is designed as a single user program and intended as such. However, collaboration with multiple users is still possible by using it with version control like Bazaar, Git, or Mercurial. You can learn more about the version control plugin here: `https://zim-wiki.org/manual/Plugins/Version_Control.html`.

One especially nice feature of Zim is that it saves your work on the fly—no need to remember to save before closing the program when you're finished.

Zim uses plain text—there's no selection of fonts available but you can make text strong (bold), add italics (emphasis), mark (highlight), and strike (Figure 1-23).

Sample text (plain)
Sample text (Strong)
Sample text (Emphasis)
Sample text (Mark)
~~Sample text~~ (strike)

Figure 1-23. *Samples of text variants in Zim*

Zim allows you to add new pages and new sub-pages and open new notebooks. This is very helpful for keeping notes organized into specific categories (Figure 1-24).

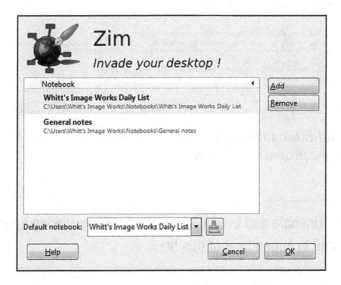

Figure 1-24. *Zim allows you to add new pages and new sub-pages and open new notebooks*

Zim Support

The *Zim User Manual* can be accessed online here: `https://zim-wiki.org/manual/Start.html`.

There is also an FAQ that addresses most, if not all, of the questions you might have about the program that is accessed from the Help tab in Zim's menu bar (Figure 1-25).

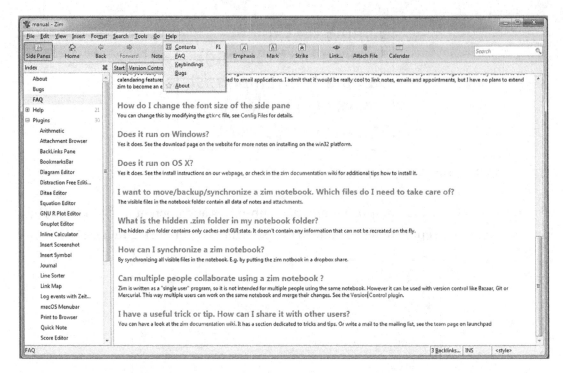

Figure 1-25. *In addition to the online user manual, there is an FAQ page that can be accessed from the program's Help tab*

Note   Microsoft Onenote and Evernote are two free note-taking applications that are briefly explored in Appendix B of this book.

GnuCash: Open Source Accounting Software

GnuCash is a powerful financial accounting software program for both personal and business use. It's designed to be easy to use yet full-featured.

- **Alternative to**: Intuit QuickBooks Advanced Plan

- **Website**: www.gnucash.org

- **License**: GNU General Public License

- **Current Version: 4.11**

- **Operating Systems**: Windows, macOS, Linux

- **Potential Savings**: $180.00 per month (compared to the Intuit QuickBooks monthly plan)

GnuCash is open source software offered under the terms of the GPL (GNU General Public License) and can be installed on multiple computers (Figure 1-26).

Figure 1-26. *GnuCash can be installed on as many computers as necessary in your business*

GnuCash is a powerful double entry–style accounting program. GnuCash has been around for quite a while (according to the GnuCash website, the first stable release was launched in 1998), so it has a long history.

It has a long list of features worth looking at. I've touched on them here the order they are shown on the website:

Main Features

- Double entry

- Checkbook-style register

- Scheduled transactions

- Reports, graphs

- Statement reconciliation
- Income/expense account types

Advanced Features

- Small business accounting features
- Multiple currencies
- Stock/mutual fund portfolios
- Online stock and mutual fund quotes

Data Storage and Exchange Features

- Experimental database support
- QIF and QFX import
- HBCI support

Other Goodies

- Multi-platform
- Localization
- Transaction finder
- Check printing
- Mortgage and loan repayment assistant
- User manual and Help

These features can be explored in greater detail here: `www.gnucash.org/features.phtml`.

When you first launch GnuCash, a Tip of the day box appears. If you like, you can toggle through it to familiarize yourself more with this program. When opening a new file, the *New Account Hierarchy Setup* wizard launches to help walk you through setting up your accounts (Figure 1-27).

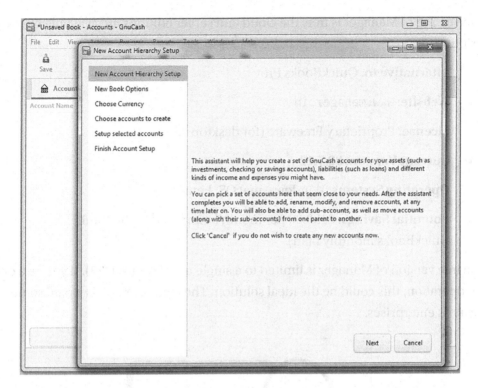

Figure 1-27. *The New Account Hierarchy Setup wizard helps walk you through setting up your accounts*

GnuCash Support

New users might find GnuCash can be a little intimidating, but there is plenty of support available. Both the *User Manual* and the *GnuCash Tutorial and Concepts Guide* can be accessed on the Documentation page of the GnuCash website: `https://gnucash.org/docs.phtml`.

There are also a number of helpful videos about GnuCash on YouTube.

Manager: Free Small Business Accounting Software

If GnuCash is a bit overwhelming, (or just a solution for a single user) then Manager might be more to your liking. It is an easy-to-use, feature-rich accounting program that the small business can appreciate. It states on the website that it is used by educators to teach accounting principles, as well as businesses and accountants. Although the desktop version of Manager is free, the cloud and server editions are available by paid subscription.

- **Alternative to**: QuickBooks Pro

- **Website**: www.manager.io

- **License**: Proprietary Freeware (for desktop version)

- **Current Version**: 22.7.12

- **Operating Systems**: Windows, macOS, Linux

- **Potential Savings**: $180.00 per month (compared to the Intuit QuickBooks monthly plan)

The free version of Manager is limited to a single user (Figure 1-28). If you're a one-person operation, this could be the ideal solution. The cloud version is a paid solution for business enterprises.

Figure 1-28. *The free version of Manager is for single users*

I actually started using this software around 2013 after installing Ubuntu (a Linux distro) on my old Dell desktop computer that had been running Windows XP. I found Manager easier to use than the old accounting software (Book Keeper) I had been using since 2006. Manager has many features, as is apparent in Table 1-1, but is still easy enough for non-accountant types such as myself.

Table 1-1. *Manager's features as shown on the software's website*

General ledger	Billable expenses	Aged payables
Cash management	Fixed asset management	Customer statements
Bank reconciliation	Capital accounts	Remittance advices
Expense claims	Profit and loss statement	Sales orders
Stock and inventory	Time and service billing	Asset register & depreciation
Capital accounts	Profit and loss statement	Comparative reporting
Accounts receivable	Balance sheet	Project-based accounting
Accounts payable	Statement of changes in equity	Bank statement importing
Estimates and quotes	Trial balance	Recurring billing
Purchase orders	VAT, GST, or sales tax	Cash-basis accounting
Billing and invoicing	Multi-currency	Accrual-basis accounting
Credit notes	Custom fields	Departmental accounting
Delivery notes	Customizable invoices	Payroll management
Sales orders	Chart of accounts	Manufacturing management
Stock and inventory	Journal entries	Email templates
Time and service billing	Aged receivables	Drill down reports

The *Manager Guides* on the website provide comprehensive, easy-to-follow instructions on getting started and using this software. There's also a community forum that can help with any issues you might have.

Manager prides itself on using a simple, clean interface that's easy to navigate. If you are well acquainted with bookkeeping, the learning curve for this program should be low enough to jump right in.

Setting up an accounting entity in Manager is an easy process by using the *Create New Business* button, or you can import a business (Figure 1-29).

Figure 1-29. Setting up your business in Manager

After these initial first steps, you can then structure your account and customize the business, such as adding your company's logo (Figure 1-30).

Figure 1-30. *You can customize your business, such as adding your company's logo*

Manager Support

Under the *Sales Invoices* menu is a *Learn how to* center. These are links to the *Guides* page that provides guidance on how to use Manager to address accounting topics (Figure 1-31).

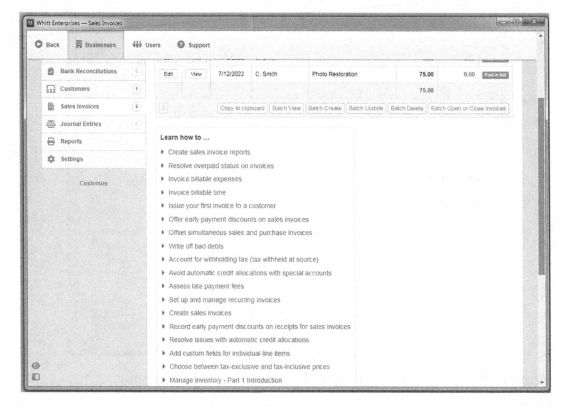

Figure 1-31. *The Learn how to center provides guidance on how to use Manager to address accounting topics*

PDF reDirect: Basic PDF Creation Freeware

This program is an excellent free program for creating PDF files. It has always been a very useful tool in my work. It is used to convert documents (such as those created in MS Word or LibreOffice) into PDF files. The professional version has more features and can be tried out for 90 days at no charge and costs $19.99 with free lifetime upgrades.

- **Alternative to**: Adobe Acrobat

- **Website**: www.expsystems.com

- **License**: Proprietary Freeware

- **Current Version:** 2.5.2

- **Operating Systems:** Windows

- **Potential Savings**: $12.99 per month subscription (compared to Acrobat Standard DC)

PDF reDirect freeware is for both personal and business use. The license allows unregistered copies of PDF reDirect freeware to be installed on multiple computers (Figure 1-32), provided they are your (or the company's) legal property.

Figure 1-32. *PDF reDirect can be installed on as many computers as necessary in your business*

If you need to create PDF files from existing documents without all of the editing abilities contained within a full-featured program like Adobe Acrobat, then PDF reDirect is really worth trying. When you're ready to convert your document into a PDF, just use the *Print* command and click PDF reDirect in the Printer options (Figure 1-33). The main downside to this program: it's only available for Windows.

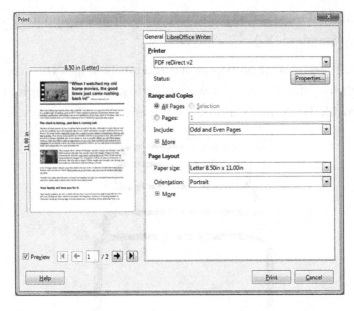

Figure 1-33.   *Select PDF reDirect in the Printer options to convert a document into a PDF*

Feature Highlights

PDF reDirect has several nice features included for being a freeware program. Here's a look at its features as they are listed on the website:

- **Create Standard PDF Files:** Create universal, standard, reliable, and secure PDF files, recognized by industries and governments around the world. Perfect for sharing information with others.

- **Easy to Use:** Compatible with virtually all Windows programs. Simply select "Print," choose the PDF reDirect virtual printer, and your PDF file is created automatically.

- **Live Preview:** Preview of PDF is displayed so you can optimize your settings on the fly.

(The Pro version provides an enhanced preview with greater detail.)

- **Optimize Quality and File Size:** Optimize your PDF files for your intended audience, from high quality for desktop publishing to creating small web-friendly files.

- **Merge PDF Files**: Combine any PDF files together like a Word report with your Excel Charts into a single PDF by dragging them to the Merge List.

- **Encrypt your PDF files**: Secure your PDF files from prying eyes by using 40 bit password protection (the Pro version uses a more secure 128 bit encryption).

- **No Pop-up Advertisements**: There are no annoying "pop-up" advertisements that appear while your PDF is being created, and there are no watermarks to deface your PDF files.

PDF reDirect also lets you control the picture quality within the printer output settings. The quality ranges from *Low* (small file size) to *High* (large file size). By default, it is set at *Very Good,* which is the second highest setting (Figure 1-34).

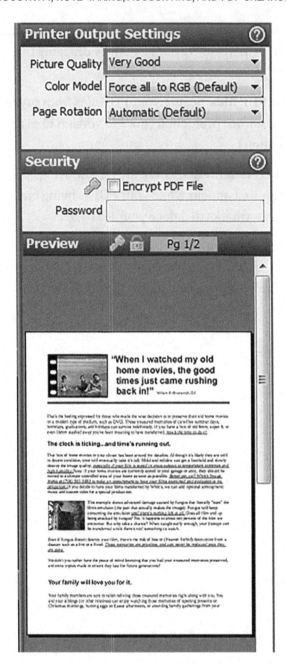

Figure 1-34. *The Picture Quality settings range from Low (small file size) to High (large file size)*

PDF reDirect Support

PDF reDirect has a good user's guide that can be found under the Support tab on the website. There is also a discussion platform under the Forum tab where users can seek help from others if they encounter problems using the program.

In addition, there is also email support from the software developers at exp@exp-systems.com.

Note   We'll take a brief look at two other free PDF software programs in Appendix B—FreePDF and PDF Slicer.

Summary

In this chapter, we looked at some useful free and free open source office productivity solutions. LibreOffice is a powerful open source suite that has grown in popularity over the years and offers a lot of features.

We looked at two free note-taking applications: Simplenote and Zim. Simplenote is a basic, easy-to-use note-taking app that can be synced across devices. Zim is great for using on a single computer and allows the user to add files (such as images) as attachments.

GnuCash and Manager are two options for free accounting software. While GnuCash is a very robust program, it can be a little intimidating for those with little or no experience using accounting software. Manager is a full-featured yet easy-to-use free accounting program that's ideal for single users.

PDF reDirect is a useful Windows-based program for converting documents into PDF files. If you don't need all of the features of Adobe Acrobat, this handy free application might just serve you well.

The next chapter looks at no-cost solutions for point-of-sale, customer relationship management, backup software, and compression software.

CHAPTER 2

Point-of-Sale, CRM, Backup, and Compression Software

This chapter looks at several solutions for handling day-to-day sales transactions, managing customer relationships, backing up data, and file compression.

Here's a quick look at the software programs covered in this chapter.

Point-of-Sale Solutions

- **Imonggo**: The free version of Imonggo offers an online point-of-sale solution for small shops, kiosks, and boutiques.

- **POS/Cash Register**: A free DOS program that can turn old PCs into fully functional cash registers.

Customer Relationship Management Solutions

- **Bitrix24**: A platform that offers CRM, collaboration, and project lists

File Backup and Compression Solutions

- **FBackup**: A freeware Windows program for backing up important ant data.

- **7Zip**: A free compression program similar to WinZip.

© Phillip Whitt 2022
P. Whitt, *Pro Freeware and Open Source Solutions for Business*, https://doi.org/10.1007/978-1-4842-8841-2_2

Imonggo (Free Version): A Point-of-Sale Utility for Small Shops or Boutiques

This is an ideal cloud-based freeware solution for small shops that keep no more than 100 different products and processes no more than 100 transactions per month. For larger shops or stores, Imonggo offers several paid options with more features.

Here are a few facts about Imonggo at a glance:

- **Competitor to**: Vend

- **Website**: www.imonggo.com/

- **License**: Proprietary Freeware

- **Current Version**: Not specified

- **Operating Systems**: Cross-platform

- **Potential Savings**: $69.00 per month

The Free Forever Imonggo plan is ideally suited to small shops with no more than 500 transactions per month and up to 100 products (Figure 2-1).

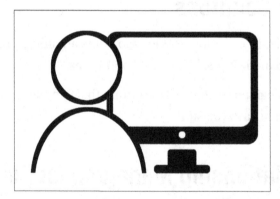

Figure 2-1. *The Free Forever Imonggo plan is best suited to single users with no more than 500 transactions per month and up to 100 products*

Feature Highlights

The *Free Forever* version of Imonggo may be the ideal solution for the small shop, kiosk, or boutique—particularly for transactions not exceeding 500 per month (Figure 2-2). For shops dealing in lower volume, higher value sales, it's an ideal free POS solution.

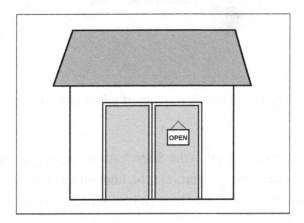

Figure 2-2. *Imonggo's Forever Free plan is for small shops with no more than 500 transactions per month*

Here's what's available in the free plan as listed on the website:

- One branch

- One user

- One hundred product limit

- Five hundred transactions per month

- Integrated inventory management

- Sales analysis

To use Imonggo, the first thing to do is to set up an account (it won't require a credit card or banking information for the free version). After your account is set up, you can go in to the *Settings* menu to set up your *Store Details, Manage Users*, etc.

You can then input your product information into the Imonggo Store: the product picture, stock number, bar code if applicable, inventory count, etc.

The *Stockroom* is where new products are created. A product picture (Figure 2-3) can be added, along with any relevant information (such as quantity in stock, product number, and item description). File sizes are limited to 64 kilobytes.

43

Figure 2-3. *A product image can be uploaded when creating a new product in the Stockroom*

The sales transaction is handled in the *Store*. You can input the customer's name, tax exempt status, sales tax amount, item(s) sold, item quantity, discount, and subtotal. Figure 2-4 is a similar representation of how an item for sale would be displayed in Imonggo's Store.

Item		Retail Price	Qty.	Discount	Subtotal
	Refurbished Dual 8 Movie Projector	275.00	1		275.00

Figure 2-4. *This graphic is similar how an item being sold is displayed in the Imonggo Store*

When receiving payment on an item, you can select the payment type: *Cash, Credit, Debit, Check, Points, Gift Certificate,* or *Others.* An invoice is generated and printed when the transaction is complete.

Note   Credit card acceptance is only available in the paid plan.

Imonggo Support

Imonggo is very easy and intuitive to use, and the website offers a great deal of support. The *Imonggo User Guide* is available by clicking the *Help* icon. There is also a link to the *Imonggo Help Index*(Figure 2-5). You can also utilize the chat feature to get help from the Imonggo team when needed.

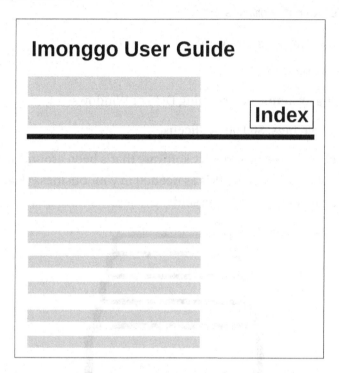

Figure 2-5. *Help can be found in the Imonggo User Guide and the link to the Imonggo Help Index*

POS/Cash Register: Turn Your Old PC into a Cash Register

Cash registers can cost several hundred dollars each. The paid commercial software for running computers as cash registers can be expensive as well, depending on its capabilities. POS/Cash Register is a free software program made available from Dale Harris Educational Software (and it *is* permitted for commercial use) that turns an older PC running DOS or Windows into a cash register. It's a DOS program and does require a little time to set up after installation. There are detailed instructions on the website, and once the program is installed and running, it's a viable way to put older computers to good use and save money in the bargain.

Here are a few facts about POS/Cash Register at a glance:

- **Alternative to**: Copper POS Software (NCH Software)

- **Website**: keyhut.com/pos.htm

- **License**: Proprietary Freeware

- **Current Version**: 7.1J

- **Operating Systems**: PCs running DOS or Windows

- **Potential Savings**: $60.00 per license

POS/Cash Register is free proprietary software that's been around since around 2001. It can be installed on as many PCs as needed in your business (Figure 2-6). The main restriction is the software can't be sold.

Figure 2-6. *POS/Cash Register can be installed on multiple PCs*

For computers running 64 bit versions of Windows XP, Vista, 7, 8, or 10, you'll need to install DOSBox (a free DOS emulator) to run POS/Cash Register. DOSBox can be downloaded here: www.dosbox.com/download.php?main=1.

Figure 2-7 shows the software's launch screen.

Figure 2-7. *The POS/Cash Register launch screen (Used with permission © Dale Harris 2022)*

Feature Highlights

POS/Cash Register is simple yet powerful. It offers a lot for a free program, and it has many fans, judging by the list of companies that use this software on the software provider's website. Here's a look at the features offered by this program:

- Works on older computers running DOS and Windows as far back as Version 3.1.

- Prints receipts on almost any printer (inkjet, laser, or specialized cash register receipt printer).

- Works with keyboard wedge scanners or USB scanners.

- Keeps track of up to 26,000 different items.

- Provides functions such as reservation and table management for any business in the food service industry.

- Keeps track of sales of up to 56 different employees.

- Records a journal of all transactions on disk as a text file.

- The program allows multiple computers to be networked together; the store can ring up sales from multiple registers at the same time, and the data from all the registers will be consolidated.

Note   Although this software doesn't directly support USB printers (such as common inkjet printers), there is a workaround solution. It's possible to configure them to work using the APRINT6.EXE file included in the software download. The detailed instructions on how to accomplish this are at `http://keyhut.com/postip4.htm#program`.

After the software has been installed, it will need to be configured by entering product categories and setting up tax rates, stock table, how to print, etc. Launching the Pos Config (Figure 2-8) program allows you to make the necessary configurations so you can use the POS/Cash Register software to ring up sales.

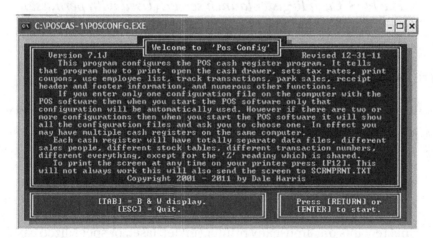

Figure 2-8. *The Pos Config program is for inputting the parameters needed to use POS/Cash Register. (Used with permission © Dale Harris 2022)*

As an option, this program keeps a journal of the daily transactions (including openings, closings, voids, etc.) on the disk as a text file. As the software's developer Dale Harris points out on his website, "You may be legally required to make and store a journal of your register transactions. In addition, it is a really good idea. The journal is your record of what was going on in your store. Was your register closed out at midday? Was that large void total from one transaction or many? How about all those refunds? Your journal will give you those answers." I can further attest to this from my own many years of experience in retail, prior to going into business for myself in 2000.

The journal can be configured to clear and reset at the beginning of each day (just make sure you've printed or archived the previous day's journal) or to keep a record of transactions on an ongoing basis. When needed, the journal can be placed into a Word processing program (such as LibreOffice or OpenOffice) and printed out (Figure 2-9).

```
              0 TEST RECEIPT
    T1   1    at    50.00ea.          50.00
    ------------------------------------------
         1
                  SUB TOTAL           50.00
         TAX1  at  7.000%              3.50
                  TOTAL TAX            3.50
                  TOTAL               53.50
    ------------------------------------------
              CASH TENDERED          100.00
              CHANGE DUE              46.50
                  05-22-2015
    ------------------------------------------
    OPEN   OPEN   OPEN   OPEN   OPEN
    TRAN = 0044    05-23-2015  12:20
    ------------------------------------------
    TX1  7.000%     52.71  0.000%       0.00
         TOTAL         52.71 TOTAL      0.00
                  TOTAL TAX:           52.71
    ------------------------------------------
              CASH SALE:        753.00   17
             CHECK SALE:          0.00    0
            CREDIT SALE:          0.00    0
             DEBIT SALE:          0.00    0
         GIFT CARD SALE:          0.00    0
                   SALE:          0.00    0
             CASH RETURN:         0.00    0
            CHECK RETURN:         0.00    0
           CREDIT RETURN:         0.00    0
            DEBIT RETURN:         0.00    0
        GIFT CARD RETURN:         0.00    0
                    RTRN:         0.00    0
              NET SALES:        753.00
              TOTAL TAX:         52.71
            GROSS SALES:        805.71
                   TIPS:          0.00
              CASH BACK:          0.00
           SUB REG CASH:        805.71
```

Figure 2-9. *A journal of all transactions is kept as a text file on the disk. (Used with permission © Dale Harris 2015)*

POS/Cash Register Support

If you have experience in working with DOS-based POS systems, you'll probably be able to use this software with relative ease. If it seems overwhelming, take the time to read over the website carefully—particularly the FAQ page and the online user manual found here:

`http://keyhut.com/posmenu.htm.`

Bitrix24: A Social Intranet, CRM Solution for Small Business

Bitrx24 is a multipurpose platform that combines collaboration, customer relationship management, and project management.

- **Alternative to**: SugarCRM

- **Website**: www.bitrix24.com

- **License**: Proprietary Freeware

- **Current Version**: Not specified

- **Operating Systems**: Web-based/cross-platform

- **Potential Savings**: $49.00 (Up to 3 users)

Bitrix24 is a web-based service, so it can be used across multiple computers and devices (Figure 2-10).

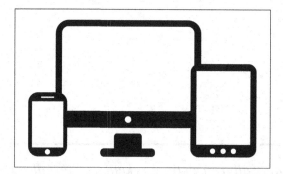

Figure 2-10. *Bitrix24 can be used across multiple computers and devices*

For many small business enterprises, the free option may be just the right solution: basic CRM, collaboration, and project/to-do lists (Figure 2-11).

Figure 2-11. *The free Bitrix24 plan is an ideal basic CRM, collaboration, and project/to-do list solution for small business*

Feature Highlights

The free version of Bitrix24 offers a fair number of features for a small enterprise. Here, we'll touch on what is available in the free plan:

- Unlimited users

- 5 GB of online storage

- Collaboration

    1. Chat

    2. HD video calls

    3. Calendar

    4. Company workspace

    5. Feed

    6. Knowledge base

- Tasks and projects

- CRM

- Drive

- Contact center

- Website builder

You can register for free using your email address, Facebook, Google, Apple Sign-In, Office 365, LiveID, or Twitter. Once your account is created, a screen appears asking you to confirm the most used items of Bitrix24 to help streamline your daily routine. It highlights *Collaboration* by default (shown in Figure 2-12).

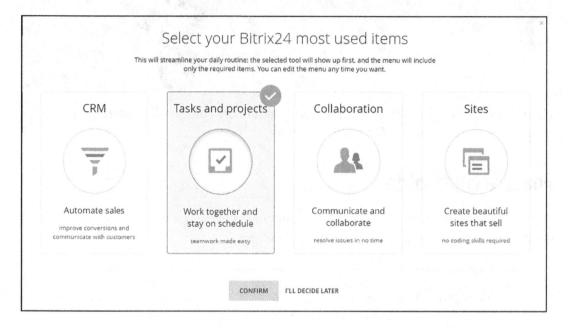

Figure 2-12. *Collaboration is highlighted by default (used with permission from Bitrix24)*

You can then set up your profile page by uploading a photo, adding your name and contact information, and filling in the About Me section and any other relevant information (Figure 2-13).

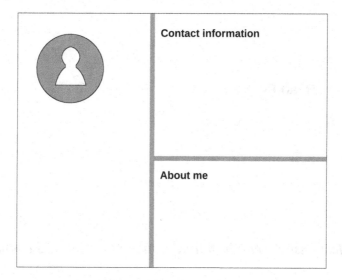

Figure 2-13. *You can upload a photo and fill out any relevant information on your profile page*

It would be a good idea at this point to watch the *Welcome to Bitrix24* video (it's only a little over 4 minutes). This will guide you on how to use the product, as well as what you can accomplish with Bitrix24. The video can be accessed here: `https://youtu.be/tAMiCw-5MJE`.

Bitrix24 Support

Clicking the Help icon opens Support24 (a page similar to the graphic shown in Figure 2-14), which provides several ways to obtain help with Bitrix24—most of the answers you will likely seek can be found in the FAQ. There is also a *Find* feature to help narrow down your search.

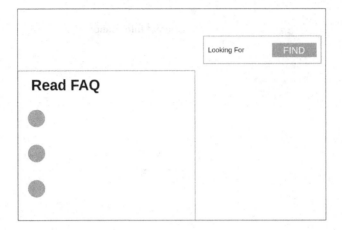

Figure 2-14. Most answers can be found in the FAQ or using the Find feature

FBackup: A Free Basic Backup Utility

We all know that protecting the data on your computer is very important—a hard drive crash or other unforeseen circumstances can effectively wipe out untold hours of hard work if the data hasn't been backed up. Sometimes, it's easy to forget to back up your files on a regular basis. FBackup is a free backup program that will help make this task easier.

> **Alternative to**: Nova BACKUP PC
>
> **Website**: www.fbackup.com/download.html
>
> **License**: Proprietary Freeware
>
> **Current Version**: 9.7
>
> **Operating Systems**: Windows
>
> **Potential Savings**: $49.95

Feature Highlights

FBackup has a number of nice features for a free program. Developed by Softland, it's a slimmed down version of the more powerful paid program Backup4all.

The detailed list of highlights can be viewed on the website—here's the quick overview (as described on the website):

- **Truly freeware**. FBackup is free for personal and commercial use.

- **Backups TO or FROM the Cloud**. With FBackup, you can back up your files and folders in the Cloud to your Google Drive or Dropbox account.

- **Standard zip compression**. FBackup uses the standard type of compression, ZIP, for storing your data.

- **Set it and forget about it**. Using the backup wizard, you have to configure what data to back up and where to save it but also when to save it.

- **Free backup plugins**. FBackup is the only freeware backup software that supports backup plugins for specific program settings and other custom data, from a list of over 100 different plugins.

- **Reliable**. FBackup is developed by the same team (Softland) and on the same platform as Backup4all.

Upon opening FBackup, you will be presented with a *Getting Started* menu (Figure 2-15). It offers the options of creating a new backup job, restoring the files from a previous backup session, and links to video tutorials, and links to various tasks.

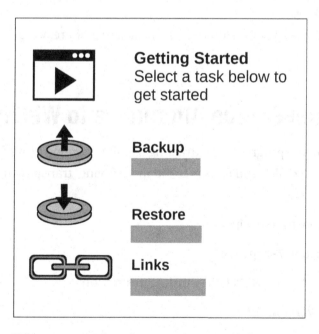

Figure 2-15. *You'll be presented with a Getting Started menu similar to this*

You can navigate to the file(s) or folder you want to backup. FBackup provides a choice of destinations to back up your files to (Figure 2-16), such as an external hard drive; disc such as CD, DVD, or Blu Ray; USB drive; a network; or online.

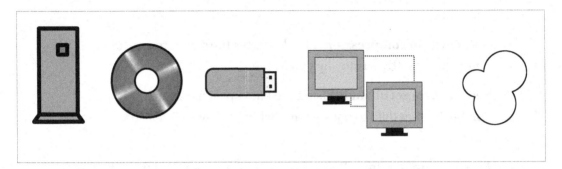

Figure 2-16. *You can select a destination to back up your files to*

FBackup offers the options of performing your backups manually as needed, or it can be set up to work automatically daily, weekly, or monthly.

FBackup Support

There is an FAQ page that provides a lot of information that can be viewed here: `www.fbackup.com/faq.html`.

In addition, there is a user forum that can be accessed here: `https://forum.fbackup.com/`.

7Zip: An Open Source Alternative to WinZip

This is a very useful free program for extracting .zip files (among other formats), as well as creating compressed files and folders to aid in archiving, transporting via email, or uploading to an FTP site.

> **Alternative to**: WinZip
>
> **Website**: `www.7-zip.org/`
>
> **License**: Mixed-GNU LGPL + unRAR restriction
>
> **Current Version**: 22.01

Operating Systems: Widows (variants available for macOS and Linux)

Potential Savings: $29.95 (WinZip Standard)

There are times that we need to transport large files and folders from one place to another. When they contain lots of data, 7Zip is a handy tool for file compression that handles several formats, making the task a bit easier.

Feature Highlights

There is a detailed list of 7Zip's features on the website, but here is a slightly abridged version:

- High compression ratio in the 7Z format.

- Some of the supported formats for packing/unpacking: 7Z, XZ, BZIP2, GZIP, TAR, ZIP, and WIM.

- Unpacks a wide variety of formats.

- For ZIP and GZIP formats, 7Zip provides a compression ratio that is 2–10% better than the ratio provided by PKZip and WinZip.

- Strong AES-256 encryption in 7z and ZIP formats.

- Self-extracting capability for 7z format.

- Integration with Windows Shell.

- Powerful File Manager.

Just one example of 7Zip's useful features is the ability to compress layered Photoshop (.PSD) or GIMP (.XCF) files. There are several layered GIMP .XCF files that total to just a little over 92 MB (Figure 2-17). As more and more folders containing layered images accumulate over time, they eventually take up lots of valuable hard drive space.

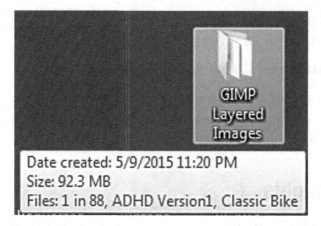

Figure 2-17. *A folder containing layered GIMP files at almost 93 MB*

Creating a compressed .ZIP folder is a matter of right-clicking the folder, navigating to 7Zip, and selecting the *Add to archive* option (Figure 2-18).

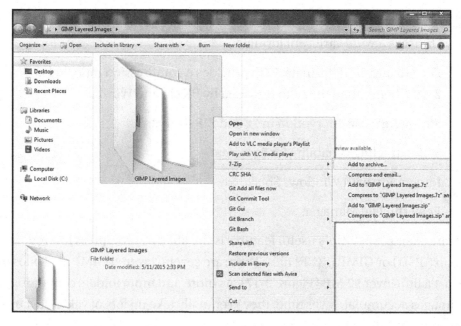

Figure 2-18. *Accessing the Add to Archive option through the dropdown menu*

A dialog box opens with numerous options such as archive format, compression level, and compression method, to name a few (Figure 2-19). There is also an option to encrypt the file, requiring a password to open.

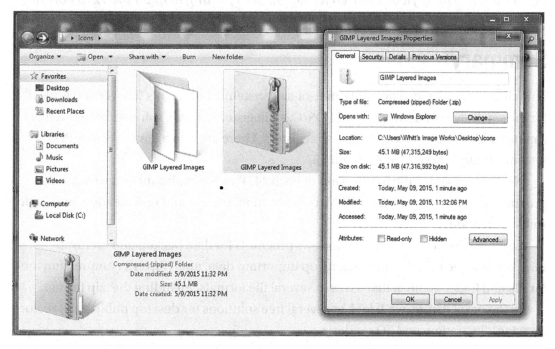

Figure 2-19. *The Add to Archive dialog box*

A zipped folder containing the layered GIMP .XCF files is created and at just over 45 MB is less than half the size of the original folder (Figure 2-20).

Figure 2-20. *The Add to Archive dialog box*

7Zip Support

The website has a support page (Figure 2-21) with a keyword search feature that lists the related topics in the *7Zip Forum*. There is also the FAQ page that is helpful. There are also a handful of instructional videos on YouTube—most of them covering the installation of 7Zip.

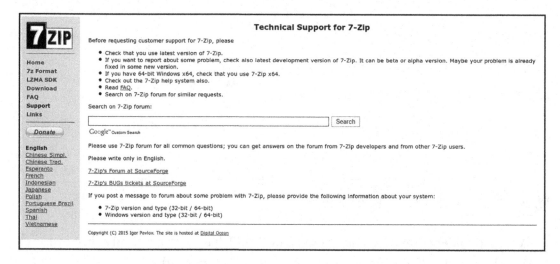

Figure 2-21. *The keyword search feature aids in finding help on the 7Zip Forum*

Summary

This chapter looks at two no-cost point-of-sale systems: Imonggo's free version is ideal for the small shop or boutique, and POS/Cash Register is a DOS software program that can turn old PCs into functioning cash registers. There are also a few other free POS systems briefly looked at in Appendix B.

Next, we looked at the free version of Bitrix24. This is a multifunction web-based program for teams. It's used for CRM, collaboration, project and task creation, and basic website creation.

Lastly, we looked at two free Windows programs for data backup and archival. FBackup is a free program for backing up important data, and 7Zip is a compression tool for file and folder archival that saves in several file formats, including the .zip format.

In the next chapter, we'll look at several free solutions for desktop publishing, vector drawing/illustration, and 3D rendering.

CHAPTER 3

Desktop Publishing, Illustration, Painting, and 3D Modeling Software

Imagine the local printshop quotes twice the amount you envisioned spending on the marketing materials you plan to use to announce your grand opening. Having marketing materials such as brochures, business cards, and flyers designed (the expensive part of the process) and printed can cut into the budget. As a business owner, wouldn't it be nice to have the means to create your own marketing materials without breaking the bank? This chapter looks at a two free desktop publishing solutions that can aid in creating your own marketing materials (such as postcards, brochures, and newsletters). If you don't need (or want) to go the route of Adobe InDesign, Microsoft Publisher, or QuarkXpress, these solutions can be perfect for small businesses with tight marketing budgets.

For creating graphic designs, there are no-cost solutions for vector illustrations and digital artwork. For the budget-minded engineer and animator, two 3D modeling programs are covered here.

Here's a quick look at the programs covered in this chapter:

- **Canva: Easy, template-based desktop publishing**

- **Scribus**: A powerful, professional-level, open source desktop publishing program for creating anything from business cards to magazines

- **Inkscape**: A powerful, professional-level vector graphics creation tool capable of stunning illustrations

© Phillip Whitt 2022
P. Whitt, *Pro Freeware and Open Source Solutions for Business*, https://doi.org/10.1007/978-1-4842-8841-2_3

- **Krita**: A drawing and painting program for creating beautiful digital artwork

- **FreeCAD**: A powerful program for rendering 3D designs of everything from small machine parts to architecture

- **Blender**: A very powerful (and complex) open source program for creating stunning 3D animations

Canva: Easy Template-Based Desktop Publishing

Canva has become a popular resource in recent years. Although it provides different pricing levels for the more advanced features (Pro and Enterprise versions), the free version has a lot to offer to the solo entrepreneur or small teams.

Here are a few facts about Canva at a glance:

- **Alternative to**: Adobe InDesign, Microsoft Publisher

- **Website**: www.canva.com

- **License**: Proprietary Freeware

- **Operating Systems**: Multiple platforms/cloud-based

- **Potential Savings**: $20.99 per month (Adobe InDesign CC subscription)

As a single user, you can sign in across multiple devices (Figure 3-1). Up to four additional users can be added at no charge.

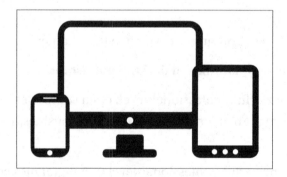

Figure 3-1. *You can sign in across multiple devices*

Feature Highlights

Here's the quick rundown of the free version of Canva's features as they're listed on the website:

- 250,000 + free templates
- 100 + design types (social media posts, presentations, letters, and more)
- Hundreds of thousands of free photos and graphics
- Invite members to your team
- Collaborate and comment in real time
- 5 GB of cloud storage

Design Capabilities

Because Canva utilizes predesigned templates, creating your work is easy—a real plus for those with no training in page layout. You can select the appropriate theme (such as business, real estate, sale flyers; there are many different ones to choose from).

You can also create designs from scratch. Starting from a blank document, you can upload your own images and add design elements and choose the right font (some fonts are only available in the paid versions of Canva). Figure 3-2 shows a fictitious real estate flyer being created from scratch.

Figure 3-2. *An example of a real estate flyer being designed from scratch*

Canva Support

Canva is easy to learn and use, but if you need help, just click the *Help* icon at the top of the menu bar. This opens the *Help Center* page—just enter the relevant word or phrase in the search feature to help narrow down your search (Figure 3-3).

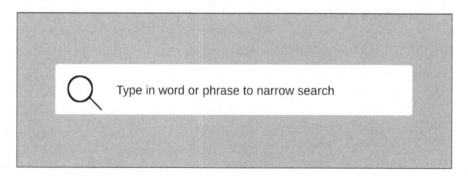

Figure 3-3. *The Help Center page offers a search feature similar to this*

Scribus: The Powerful, Professional, Open Source Desktop Publishing Program

Scribus is an extremely capable program, but it has a steep learning curve for beginners. It was originally written for Linux but is currently available for macOS X, OS2, and Windows. If you have experience with desktop publishing software such as Adobe InDesign or QuarkXpress, Scribus should be relatively easy to learn, but it does differ in some respects to these programs.

Here are a few facts about Scribus at a glance:

- **Alternative to**: Adobe InDesign, QuarkXpress

- **Website**: `wiki.scribus.net`

- **License**: GPL

- **Current Version**: 1.4.8

- **Operating Systems**: Windows, macOS, Linux

- **Potential Savings**: $20.99 per month (Adobe InDesign CC subscription)

Scribus is an open source program, so it can be installed on as many computers as needed (Figure 3-4).

Figure 3-4. *Scribus can be installed on as many computers as needed*

Scribus can help you create impressive documents, everything from business cards to magazines. I use Scribus for creating my own marketing materials, such as two-panel pamphlets and flyers. Figure 3-5 shows a sample of the inside pages of a pamphlet I designed using Scribus.

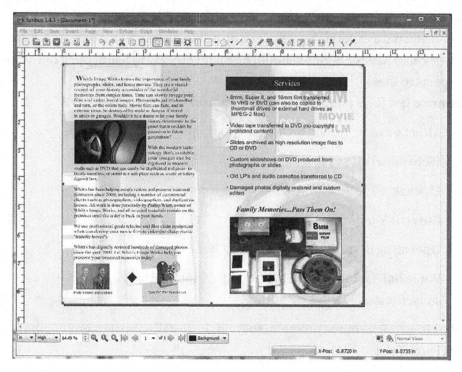

Figure 3-5.   *The inside pages of a pamphlet I designed using Scribus*

Feature Highlights

Scribus boasts a plethora of features that make this a professional-quality application. The following is just a quick rundown:

- CMYK colors

- Spot color support

- ICC color management

- Versatile PDF creation

- Vector drawing tools

- Emulation of color blindness

Design Capabilities

Scribus is a pro-class application that allows the user to design documents (mainly) from scratch. Upon launch, you'll be presented with a dialog box to select the document type, page size, orientation, etc. Documents are created in Scribus by using frames for text and images (Figure 3-6); there are also design elements such as shapes and tools for creating vector-based images.

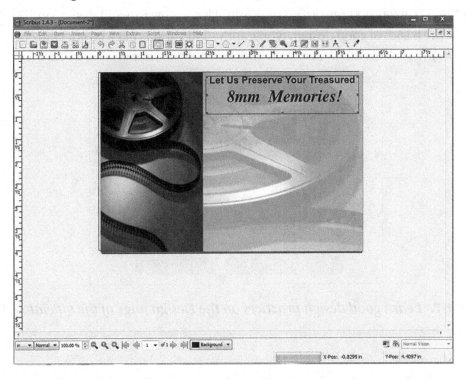

Figure 3-6. *Scribus employs text and image frames for designing documents*

Note   Prior to installing Scribus, it's a good idea to install Ghostscript (an interpreter for PostScript and Encapsulated PostScript files) from www.ghostscript.com. Although Scribus might work just fine without it, it is necessary to import EPS files and for the Print Preview to function.

For those that prefer not to build documents from the ground up, there are several templates that can be downloaded from Pling Artwork: www.free-artwork.org/browse?cat=196&tag=scribus.

Scribus Support

Scribus is very popular, and there is a wealth of support for it. The user manual on the official website will take you completely through the functionality of this program. There are quite a few video tutorials on YouTube that can help get you up and running.

If you are new to desktop publishing and really want to sink your teeth into it using Scribus, I recommend studying the Design page of the Scribus website (`http://wiki.scribus.net/canvas/Category:Design`). You'll learn how to avoid design problems, as well as the basics of good design, typography, and various page layout concepts (Figure 3-7).

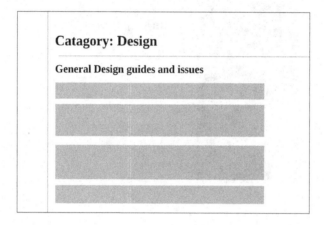

Figure 3-7. *Learn good design practices on the Design page of the official Scribus website*

Vectr: A Free, Basic Online Vector Drawing Program

This program is ideal for those new to vector drawing and who don't need the advanced features found in Adobe Illustrator or Corel Draw. Even though it is easy to learn, it can still yield impressive results.

Here are a few facts about Serif Draw Plus SE at a glance:

- **Alternative to**: Adobe Illustrator

- **Website**: `https://vectr.com/`

- **License**: Proprietary Freeware

- **Operating Systems**: Cross-platform
- **Potential Savings**: $20.99 per month (Adobe Illustrator CC subscription)

Because Vectr is web-based, it can be used across multiple computer platforms (Figure 3-8).

Figure 3-8. *Vectr is web-based and can be used on multiple platforms*

Feature Highlights

Vectr helps make it easy to create vector illustrations, which can be scaled up without losing quality. Here are the main highlights of this program:

- Add pages
- Layers
- Elements (predrawn images such as arrows, geometric shapes, etc.)
- Shapes (geometric shapes, callouts, icons, etc.)
- Pen tool
- Pencil tool
- Text

- Upload image
- Settings

Graphics Creation

Vectr is ideal for creating simple drawings (in the right hands, it's capable of more complex artwork). Figure 3-9 shows a simple illustration of a billiard ball using shapes and text.

Figure 3-9. *A simple illustration created using Vectr*

The example in Figure 3-10 is a predrawn shape (filled in with light gray by default) and then filled in with black and several elements to give the lens more detail.

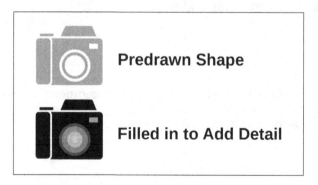

Figure 3-10. *A comparison of the default shape and then filled in with black and several circular elements to give the lens more detail*

Vectr Support

At the time of this writing, the developers of Vectr are in the process of adding a User Guide and Tutorial to the website. For now, there are a number of video tutorials on YouTube, although they are several years old.

You can view a short introductory video here: `https://youtu.be/CnSRzM91FYY`.

Inkscape: Pro-quality Open Source Vector Drawing Software

Inkscape is a powerful (and popular) vector-based drawing program used for creating scalable graphics. It's used by illustrators, designers, and web designers.

Here are a few facts about Inkscape at a glance:

- **Alternative to**: Adobe Illustrator

- **Website**: `www.inkscape.org`

- **License**: GPL

- **Current Version**: 1.1.2

- **Operating Systems**: Windows, macOS, Linux

- **Potential Savings**: $20.99 per month (Adobe Illustrator CC subscription)

Inkscape is free and open source under the terms of the GNU General Public License, so it can be installed on as many computers as needed (Figure 3-11).

Figure 3-11. *Inkscape is free, open source software and can be installed on as many computers as needed*

Inkscape has a wide array of tools, effects, simulated materials, and textures to create anything from simple to complex designs. Figure 3-12 shows a camera that was rendered using Inkscape. The Gallery page on the Inkscape website showcases many examples of outstanding work created by digital artists using this software.

Figure 3-12. *An illustration of a camera created using Inkscape*

Feature Highlights

Inkscape offers many features one would expect from a full-featured illustration program
such as the following:

- Flexible drawing tools

- Broad file format compatibility

- Powerful text tool

- Bezier and Spiro curves

These are just a few. While Inkscape is not yet in the same league as Adobe
Illustrator, it is a feature-packed program.

Graphics Creation

Inkscape offers a high degree of control over the elements (called objects in Inkscape) used to create your work. In the hands of a good designer or illustrator, Inkscape is capable of rendering very detailed and realistic drawings. In Figure 3-13, the billiard is comprised of objects such as circles and ellipses. The Fill and Stroke dialog allows you to control the type of fill (solid color, gradient, etc.). Objects can be blurred, and the degree of opacity controlled. I was able to create a reasonably realistic highlight reflecting from the ball, as well as a shadow underneath.

Figure 3-13. *Objects that comprise illustrations can be edited for added realism, such as blurring the reflection slightly*

Note   Inkscape can be demanding of your computer's resources, so the more RAM and processing power your machine has, the better.

It's possible to add realism to objects by applying various filters to them. Inkscape offers a wide variety, many of which add a 3D look. The examples in Figure 3-14 are just a few of the many available in Inkscape.

Figure 3-14. *Applying filters to objects created in Inkscape adds a degree of realism*

Note   Inkscape's native file format is the Inkscape SVG (*Scalable Vector Graphics*) format, but it is capable of exporting your work in a number of other file formats.

Inkscape Support

Inkscape's FAQ page on the official website is a great place to start. There are a few books available on Amazon geared toward the beginner. There are tons of video tutorials on YouTube, which can be very useful for the beginner. The vibrant Inkscape Community can also be a valuable resource for learning this powerful program.

The Inkscape Beginner's Guide is perfect for new users and can be accessed here: https://inkscape-manuals.readthedocs.io/en/latest/.

Krita: The Powerful Open Source Digital Drawing and Painting Program

For those who love to draw and paint and would like to translate their skills into digital art creation, Krita is a full-featured program designed to do just that. Take some time to look through the Gallery page on the website to see some of the incredible art that has been created by digital artists using Krita.

Here are a few facts about Krita at a glance:

- **Alternative to**: Corel Painter

- **Website**: https://krita.org/

- **License**: GPL

- **Current Version**: 5.0.6

- **Operating Systems**: Windows , macOS, Linux 64 bit AppImage

- **Potential Savings**: $429.00 (Corel Painter)

Krita is free and open source under the terms of the GNU General Public License, so it can be installed on as many computers as needed (Figure 3-15).

Figure 3-15.   *Krita is free, open source software and can be installed on as many computers as needed*

Krita is perfect for creating digital art using the wide array of tools and brushes at your disposal (Figure 3-16). For those with experience in programs like Corel Painter, Art Weaver, and other similar painting applications, the learning curve should be relatively low.

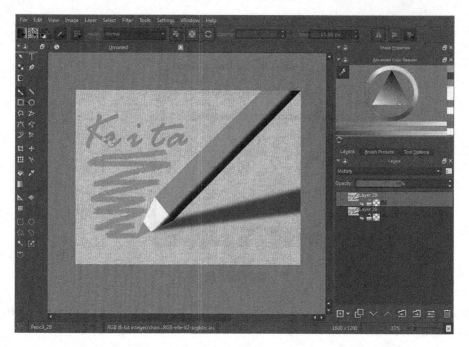

Figure 3-16. *Krita offers a wide array of drawing and painting tools*

Feature Highlights

Krita is a feature-packed program with more features than I can cover in this book. To get acquainted with Krita, a good place for beginners to start is the Getting Started page: https://docs.krita.org/en/user_manual/getting_started.html.

Document Creation

When Krita is launched, you are presented with the option to open a recent document or create a custom document and an assortment of template options, such as comic book, DSLR, film, and texture (Figure 3-17).

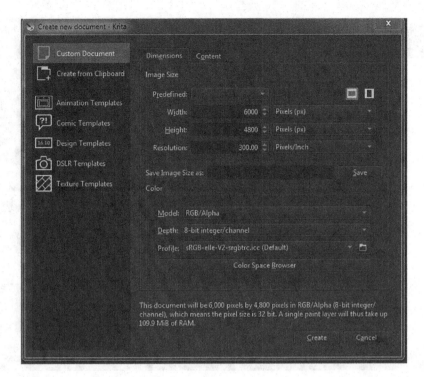

Figure 3-17. *The new document creation window that opens upon launching Krita*

Brush Presets

There are many brush presets in Krita—airbrush, felt-tip drawing markers, pens, pencils, erasers—just about anything one would need to create stunning artwork. Brushes can be accessed by right-clicking in the workspace or from the palette in the lower right hand side of the window (Figure 3-18).

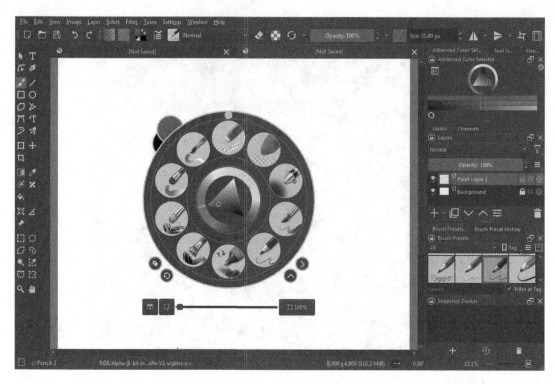

Figure 3-18. *Krita has a wide variety of brush presets and can be accessed by right-clicking in the workspace or from the palette in the lower right-hand side of the window*

Tip   For those who are new to digital painting, you may want to use a graphics/ drawing tablet. It gives you better control when applying brush strokes.

Krita Support

As previously mentioned, the *Getting Started* page is the first place to familiarize yourself with Krita. When you're ready to get to work, you'll probably want to access the *User Manual* here: `https://docs.krita.org/en/user_manual.html`.

There are also numerous videos on YouTube to help you get underway with Krita.

Note   In addition to Krita, there are other free drawing applications worth evaluating. Appendix B covers MyPaint and Sumopaint.

FreeCAD: Open Source Parametric 3D Modeling Software

FreeCAD is a popular open source program for rendering 2D and 3D drawings, and it is particularly useful for mechanical design. FreeCAD has been around for a while but is constantly evolving, thanks to an active community of developers. Although it's not in the same league as the commercial counterparts (such as AutoCAD), it still offers a ton of features and is suitable for commercial use.

Here are a few facts about FreeCAD at a glance:

- **Alternative to**: Autodesk AutoCAD

- **Website**: www.freecadweb.org

- **License**: GPL

- **Current Version**: 0.20.0

- **Operating Systems**: Windows, macOS, Linux

- **Potential Savings**: $1865.00 per year (Autodesk AutoCAD subscription)

FreeCAD is free and open source under the terms of the GNU General Public License, so it can be installed on as many computers as needed (Figure 3-19).

Figure 3-19. *FreeCAD is free, open source software and can be installed on as many computers as needed*

FreeCAD is capable of rendering 3D models for those involved in mechanical drawing, engineering, or even students studying computer-aided design. It can render everything from simple parts (Figure 3-20) to highly detailed systems.

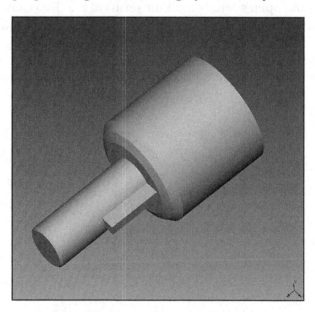

Figure 3-20. *A machine part rendered in FreeCAD*

Note   Aspiring engineers or small start-up firms could potentially save thousands of dollars annually by using FreeCAD. Even if a firm requires a commercial application like AutoCAD on one or two computers, installing FreeCAD on the remaining computers could result in huge savings overall on licensing fees.

Feature Highlights

FreeCAD has a long list of features, which can be explored in depth on the website on the *Features* list page. Here's a quick rundown of some of them:

- *A full parametric model*: Changes can be recalculated as needed while work is in progress.

- *Modular architecture*: The core application's functionality can be expanded with plug-ins.

- *Sketcher mode*: This allows sketching 2D geometry with constraint-solving capabilities.

- *A Robot module*: This allows the study of robot movements.

- *An Architecture module*: This allows a BIM (Building Information Modeling) type workflow.

- *Drawing sheets*: This allows you to put 2D views of your 3D models on a sheet.

A particularly useful feature of FreeCAD is a concept in which tools are grouped by *workbenches* (Figure 3-21). This allows only the tools needed for a specific task to be displayed. The workspace stays uncluttered and helps the program to load faster.

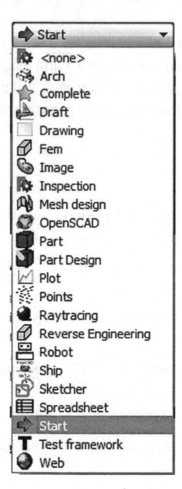

Figure 3-21. *FreeCAD utilizes workbenches, allowing only the tools for a specific task to be displayed*

Drafting Capabilities

The Draft workbench (Figure 3-22) allows you to draw simple 2D objects, which can be modified afterward. The Draft workbench provides a snapping system and several utilities to manage objects and settings.

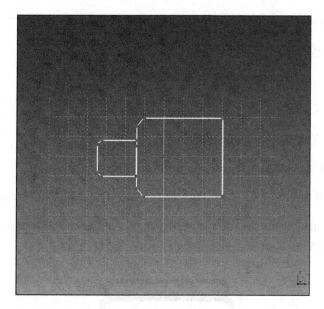

Figure 3-22. *The Draft workbench allows the creation of simple 2D objects*

FreeCAD Support

The best place to start with this program is the *About FreeCAD* page (this provides a good general overview of this program): https://wiki.freecad.org/About_FreeCAD.

After reading the About FreeCAD page, you can proceed to the Tutorials page found here: https://wiki.freecad.org/Tutorials.

There are numerous videos on YouTube; this is a good introductory video for beginners to view: https://youtu.be/u8otDF_C_fw.

Blender: The Ultimate Open Source 3D Creation Software

Blender is a free and open source professional 3D creation application. Like FreeCAD, Blender can create 3D renderings. The primary difference is that Blender is geared mainly toward animation creation for motion pictures and gaming (but it is used for other purposes).

Here are a few facts about Blender at a glance:

- **Alternative to**: Autodesk Maya

- **Website**: www.blender.org

- **License**: GPL

- **Current Version**: 3.2.1

- **Operating Systems**: Windows, macOS, Linux

- **Potential Savings**: $1785.00 per year (Autodesk Maya subscription)

Blender is free and open source under the terms of the GNU General Public License, so it can be installed on as many computers as needed (Figure 3-23).

Figure 3-23. *Blender is free, open source software and can be installed on as many computers as needed*

Blender is a very popular software program in the world of 3D animation. In fact, it's so powerful and feature-packed that it's hard to believe that it is a free program. It's been used to make several animated motion pictures, and it is a very robust program. It is capable of rendering water simulations, textures, and other materials with incredible realism.

Note   There have been several animated motion pictures created using Blender. The one entitled *Big Buck Bunny* (2008) is a short animated film featuring Liam Neeson and voice-over actor Frank Welker.

Feature Highlights

Blender, like any high-powered software program, has a long list of features, all of which are on the Features page of the Blender website. Here's a quick look at the key features available in Blender:

- Photo-realistic rendering
- Fast modeling
- Realistic materials
- Fast rigging
- Animation toolset
- Sculpting
- Fast UV unwrapping
- Full compositor
- Amazing simulations
- Game creation
- Camera and object tracking
- Library of extensions
- Video editing
- File formats
- Flexible interface

Rendering Capabilities

Blender is capable of very realistic and detailed 3D models. The best way to see what can be created is to spend some time on the website. Of course, everything begins somewhere. Masterpieces created using Blender start out as basic elements, which are then combined and manipulated (Figure 3-24).

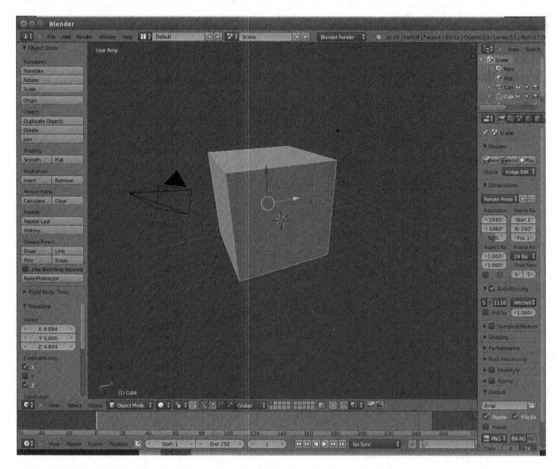

Figure 3-24. *Masterpieces created in Blender start out as basic elements*

Blender Support

Complex is probably a gross understatement to sum up Blender. If you're a beginner, you'll likely be overwhelmed by all of the bells and whistles. Fortunately, there is ample support and documentation on the website to start the learning process. A good starting point is the *Tutorials* page of the Blender website: www.blender.org/support/tutorials/.

There are also numerous videos on the Blender Foundation's YouTube channel: www.youtube.com/c/BlenderFoundation.

Summary

In this chapter, you looked at some useful free and open source solutions for desktop publishing. Canva utilizes templates making it easy for those with no experience in desktop design to create effective materials. Scribus is a powerful, open source desktop publishing program capable of producing impressive documents ranging from brochures and flyers to magazines. Scribus is used by enthusiasts and professionals the world over.

We covered two illustration programs: Vectr and Inkscape. Vectr is a web-based application that utilizes predrawn shapes and icons, helping beginners quickly create vector-based illustrations and graphics. Inkscape is a professional-quality, open source program with tons of features. Inkscape is capable of producing stunning graphics.

Krita is a powerful, open source drawing and painting program capable of producing digital artwork by simulating traditional media. Two more drawing programs that are not in this chapter but touched on in Appendix B are MyPaint and Sumo Paint.

FreeCAD and Blender are two complex and powerful open source programs design for 3D model creation. FreeCAD is used primarily for mechanical drawing, architecture, and engineering. Blender is mainly used for creating 3D animations for motion pictures and game creation, although it can be used for other purposes.

The next chapter will look at several no-cost photo editing programs. The programs range from easy-to-use, entry-level programs to advanced, professional-level programs.

CHAPTER 4

Photo Editing Software

When you think of photo editing, Adobe Photoshop probably springs to mind. It is the industry standard and the ultimate in photo editing software. There are many professionals who use Adobe products because they are involved with very high-end print production and photography or just locked into an Adobe workflow. However, for many small business owners, freelance photographers, and designers, Photoshop is either too expensive (even at $20.99 per month for the subscription service, people don't like the idea of "renting" software), or it's just overkill.

Since digital photography has become mainstream, the ability to work with digital images is an important aspect for most businesses. Fortunately, there are many no-cost photo editing programs to help you get best out of your digital photos. This chapter looks at several photo editing programs, ranging from simple (applying effects automatically) to professional level (with a wide range of editing capabilities).

Here's a quick look at the programs we'll cover in this chapter:

- **PhotoScape**: An entry-level photo editing tool that offers minor, easy photo corrections and a wealth of special effects filters

- **Paint.NET**: A lightweight yet powerful photo editor for Windows with graphics creation capability

- **GIMP**: A professional photo editing and graphics creation program almost in the same league as Adobe Photoshop

- **Pixlr**: A family of cloud-based and mobile applications for photo editing and adding special effects

- **Darktable**: A program for processing RAW images (RAW is the uncompressed format used by many higher-end cameras)

- **FotoSketcher**: A program that automatically creates art from photographic images

© Phillip Whitt 2022
P. Whitt, *Pro Freeware and Open Source Solutions for Business*, https://doi.org/10.1007/978-1-4842-8841-2_4

Note   A helpful photography-related website worth checking out is `www.opensourcephotography.org`.

PhotoScape: An Easy-to-Use Photo Editor for Beginners

If you use Windows or macOS and require a program to perform basic photo editing functions such as cropping, red-eye removal, adjusting contrast, etc., then PhotoScape is really worth trying out, particularity for those with little or no previous photo editing experience.

Here are a few facts about PhotoScape at a glance:

- **Alternative to**: Adobe Photoshop, Photoshop Elements

- **Website**: `www.photoscape.org`

- **License**: Proprietary Freeware

- **Current Version**: PhotoScape X

- **Operating Systems**: Windows, macOS (for Windows XP, Vista, 7, or 8, use PhotoScape 3.7)

- **Potential Savings**: $20.99 per month (Photoshop subscription)

Upon launching the program, you'll be greeted with a menu that makes it easy to navigate to the desired function (Figure 4-1).

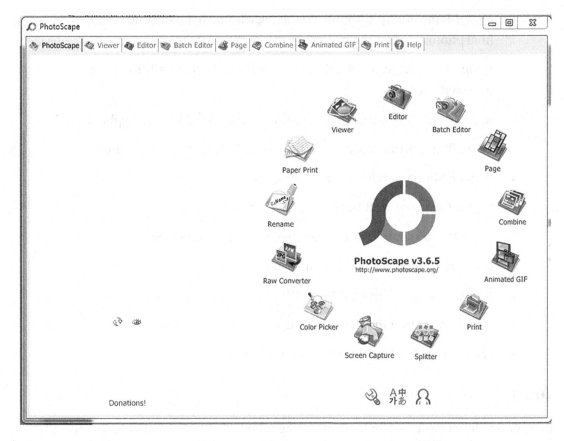

Figure 4-1. *PhotoScape makes it easy to navigate to the desired function upon launching. (Used with permission © Mooiitech 2015)*

Feature Highlights

Even though PhotoScape could be considered an entry-level editing application (it only has a few editing tools compared to other programs), it does offer many useful functions.

Here are PhotoScape's features as listed on the software provider's website:

- *Viewer*: View photos in your folder; create a slideshow.

- *Editor*: Resizing, brightness and color adjustment, white balance, backlight correction, frames, balloons, mosaic mode, adding text, drawing pictures, cropping, filters, red-eye removal, blooming, paint brush, clone stamp, and effect brush.

- *Batch editor*: Batch edit multiple photos.

- *Page*: Merge multiple photos on the page frame to create one final photo.

- *Combine*: Attach multiple photos vertically or horizontally to create one final photo.

- *Animated GIF*: Use multiple photos to create a final animated photo.

- *Print*: Print portrait shots, carte de visites (CDV), passport photos.

- *Splitter*: Slice a photo into several pieces.

- *Screen Capture*: Capture your screenshot and save it.

- *Color Picker*: Zoom in on images; search and pick a color.

- *Rename*: Change photo file names in batch mode.

- *Raw Converter*: Convert RAW to JPG.

- *Paper Print*: Print lined, graph, music, and calendar paper.

- *Face Search*: Find similar faces on the Internet.

Tools

PhotoScape has a basic toolset for performing minor retouching tasks and applying effects. One of the more useful tools is the *Clone Stamp* tool. It is used for removing defects and unwanted objects or for duplicating certain parts of the image. I used it to remove the plastic pail behind the dog (Figure 4-2).

Figure 4-2. *Using the Clone Stamp tool to remove the plastic pail behind the dog (Used with permission © Mooiitech 2015)*

The *Effect Brush* is another useful tool. It can lighten or darken portions of an image (much like the dodge and burn tools in Photoshop), soften and blur areas of an image, and apply a few fun effects as well. The other tools are the *Paint Brush, Color Picker, Mosaic, Mole Removal,* and *Screen Scroll.*

Filters

While PhotoScape just has a basic toolset, it has a rich assortment of *filters*, which are functions that modify the appearance of an image. There are many effects that can be created using PhotoScape's filters. There are filters that can modify images to look like paintings or drawings, or you can apply various tones, just to name a few. Filters can give images a certain look and feel. To give the image of the cowboy a look more consistent with the Old West, I first applied a sepia tone and then one of the *Vintage Effect* filters (Figure 4-3).

Figure 4-3. *Before and after comparison*

Objects

PhotoScape lets you have fun with your images by allowing you to add *Objects* to your images. The Objects in the Office category (Figure 4-4) are useful for enhancing images that will be used in business communications, such as newsletters or marketing pieces. The Christmas-themed Objects come in handy when making Christmas cards, holiday-themed images, etc.

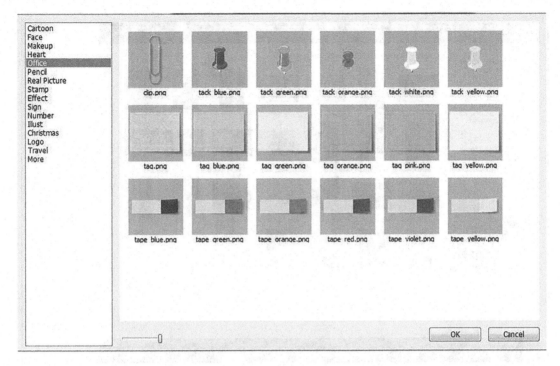

Figure 4-4. *Have fun with your images using PhotoScape Objects. (Used with permission © Mooiitech 2015)*

PhotoScape Support

A great starting point for learning PhotoScape is the documentation on the *Help* page of the website. The Intro video gives a quick tour of the functions of PhotoScape (Figure 4-5). You can access even more helpful videos under the software's *Help* tab. There are also a number of PhotoScape tutorials on YouTube.

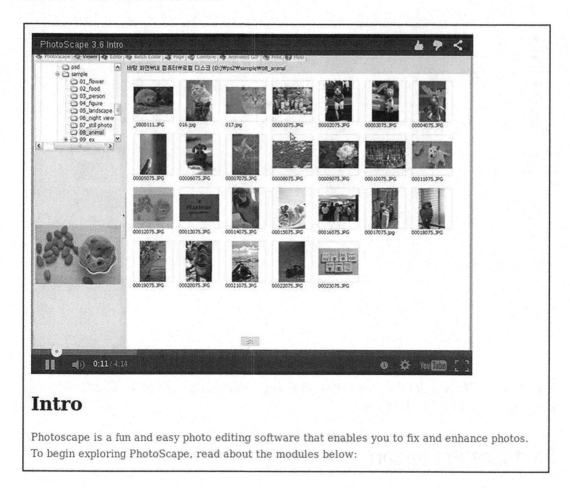

Figure 4-5. *The Intro video on the Help page of PhotoScape's website (Used with permission © Mooiitech 2015)*

Paint.NET: Basic Image Editing for Windows

Paint.NET is a popular, no-cost editing program for Windows-based computers. Although still easy enough for beginners to jump into and master with a little practice, it's not quite as automated as PhotoScape. Anyone with experience using commercial image editing software will have a very low learning curve using this program and will pick it up in no time.

Here are a few facts about Paint.NET at a glance:

- **Alternative to:** Adobe Photoshop, Photoshop Elements

- **Website:** `www.getpaint.net`

- **License:** Proprietary Freeware

- **Current Version:** 4.3.11

- **Operating Systems:** Windows

- **Potential Savings:** $20.99 per month (Photoshop subscription)

Paint.NET is freeware. Although it can't be sold (nor can the source code be altered), it can be installed on as many computers as needed (Figure 4-6).

Figure 4-6. *Paint.NET can be installed on as many computers as needed*

Paint.NET has an interface that is somewhat reminiscent of Photoshop, but its unique focus is on being intuitive and easy to learn (Figure 4-7). Many of the functions use keyboard shortcuts that will make work faster and more efficient.

Figure 4-7. *The Paint.NET interface is designed to be intuitive and easy to learn. (Used with permission © Rick Brewster 2015)*

Feature Highlights

Paint.NET offers an impressive array of features and functionality for a free program. The website states that "It is one of the fastest free photo editors for Windows, with a capable feature set that stops just short of some of the professional manipulation tools."

These are the features as described on the software provider's website:

- **Simple, intuitive, and innovative user interface**: Every feature and user interface element was designed to be immediately intuitive and quickly learnable without assistance. In order to handle multiple images easily, Paint.NET uses a tabbed document interface. The tabs display a live thumbnail of the image instead of a text description. This makes navigation very simple and fast. The interface is also enhanced for Aero Glass if you are using Windows 7 or Vista.

- **Performance**: Extensive work has gone into making Paint.NET the fastest image editor available. Whether you have a netbook with a power-conscious Atom CPU or a Dual Intel Xeon workstation with eight blazingly fast processing cores, you can expect Paint.NET to start up quickly and be responsive to every mouse click.

- **Layers**: Usually only found on expensive or complicated professional software, layers form the basis for a rich image composition experience. You may think of them as a stack of transparency slides that, when viewed together at the same time, form one image.

- **Active online community**: Paint.NET has an online forum with a friendly, passionate, and ever-expanding community. Be sure to check out the constantly growing list of tutorials and plug-ins.

- **Automatically updated**: Updates are free, and they contain new features, performance improvements, and bug fixes. Upgrading to the latest version is very simple, requiring only two clicks of the mouse.

- **Special effects**: Many special effects are included for enhancing and perfecting your images. Everything from blurring, sharpening, red-eye removal, distortion, noise, and embossing are included. Also included is a unique 3D rotate/zoom effect that makes it very easy to add perspective and tilting. Adjustments are also included, which help you tweak an image's brightness, contrast, hue, saturation, curves, and levels. You can also convert an image to black-and-white or sepia-toned.

- **Powerful tools**: Paint.NET includes simple tools for drawing shapes, including an easy-to-use *Curve* tool for drawing splines or Bezier curves. The *Gradient* tool, new for 3.0, has been cited as an innovative improvement over similar tools provided by other software. The facilities for creating and working with selections are powerful yet simple enough to be picked up quickly. Other powerful tools include the *Magic Wand* for selecting regions of similar color and the *Clone Stamp* for copying or erasing portions of an image. There is also a simple text editor, a tool for zooming, and a *Recolor* tool.

- **Unlimited History**: Everybody makes mistakes, and everybody changes their mind. To accommodate this, *every* action you perform on an image is recorded in the History window and may be undone. Once you've undone an action, you can also redo it. The length of the history is only limited by available disk space.

- **Free**: Paint.NET doesn't cost a dime!

Editing Capabilities

Paint.NET can handle a number of editing tasks ranging from simple to fairly complex. It's great for touching up images, making composite images, and correcting color and exposure, to name a few. It offers several tools for correcting exposure and color, but the most advanced is the *Curves* dialog, which is used to correct tonal quality and color with precision (Figure 4-8). Curves is a high-end tool usually found only in more complex image editors.

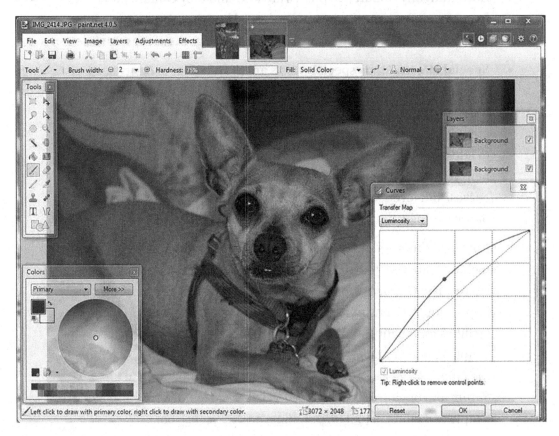

Figure 4-8. *Correcting exposure using Curves (Used with permission © Rick Brewster 2015)*

Paint.NET has a decent assortment of editing tools (although it lacks a few, such as the Dodge and Burn tools). Among them is a *Clone Stamp* tool that is essential in many image editing tasks. Figure 4-9 demonstrates its usefulness by digitally removing the date stamp from the lower right portion of the image.

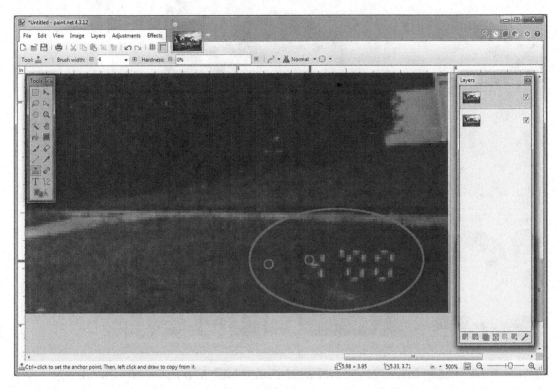

Figure 4-9. *Removing the date stamp using the Clone Stamp tool (Used with permission © Rick Brewster 2015)*

Paint.NET employs the use of *layers,* which allows for the placement of graphical elements without directly affecting the original image. The layers in Paint.NET have several *blending modes* to choose from. Blending modes determine how the layer's pixels interact with those of the image below. Additionally, the opacity/transparency of each layer can be controlled. This allows the use of advanced editing techniques, such as adding color to a monochrome image (Figure 4-10).

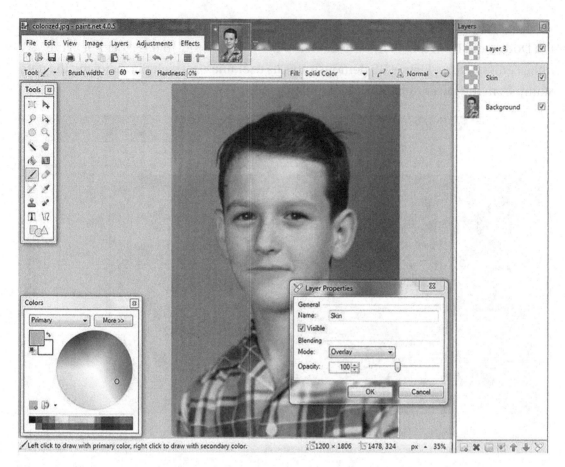

Figure 4-10. *Using layers to add a hand-tinted look to a monochrome image (Used with permission © Rick Brewster 2015)*

By using a dedicated layer for each element colorized, there is a greater degree of editing control. The end result is a monochrome image with a reasonably natural, hand-tinted look added (Figure 4-11).

Figure 4-11. *Before and after comparison*

Note   There are quite a few useful plug-ins that are available to extend Paint. NET's capabilities. Plug-ins are software add-ons written by the Paint.NET community, and information about them is available on the Forum section of the software provider's website.

Graphics Creation

In addition to editing digital photos, Paint.NET is capable of creating useful graphics from the ground up. While it's not in the league of more full-featured programs, it's still powerful enough to render eye-catching art (Figure 4-12). There are several predesigned drawing shapes (arrows, polygons, etc.) that will aid in creating graphics.

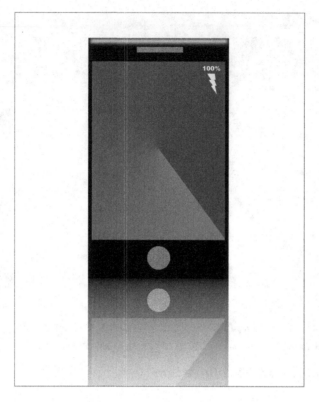

Figure 4-12. *Paint.NET is capable of creating eye-catching raster graphics*

Paint.NET Support

Paint.NET's ease of use makes it a popular program, and based on what I've read while perusing the forums, users of this program seem quite passionate about it. There is a great deal of information in the *Forums* section, including a *Discussions and Questions* page. YouTube also has a number of tutorials aimed at the beginner. You can probably learn everything you want to about this program from the information available on the Web. For those who want to dig even deeper, check out my book *Practical Paint.NET* (also by Apress Publishing).

GIMP: The Premier Open Source Image Editor

GIMP (which stands for GNU Image Manipulation Program) is arguably the most powerful, full-featured, no-cost image editing program. Currently in version 2.10.32, it has been around since the mid-1990s. It's very popular and enjoys a huge amount of support from the open source community. It's still not in the same strata as Adobe Photoshop, but it comes close enough for many users.

Here are a few facts about GIMP at a glance:

- **Alternative to**: Adobe Photoshop, Photoshop Elements

- **Website**: `www.gimp.org`

- **License**: GPL

- **Current Version**: 2.10.32

- **Operating Systems**: Windows, Mac OX, Linux, and Unix derivatives

- **Potential Savings**: $20.99 per month (Photoshop subscription)

GIMP is free and open source software and can be installed on as many computers as needed (Figure 4-13).

Figure 4-13. *GIMP can be installed on as many computers as needed*

GIMP is an extremely capable image editor loaded with many high-end features normally only seen in expensive commercial editors. It's used by enthusiasts and professionals worldwide. Figure 4-14 shows the GIMP interface.

Figure 4-14. *The dark-themed GIMP interface*

Feature Highlights

GIMP offers a dazzling array of high-end features. Being the powerful program that it is, it isn't as user friendly to the beginner as PhotoScape or Paint.NET. However, if you are willing to invest the time it takes to gain proficiency, it will handle just about any image editing task. Here are the features as described on the official GIMP website:

- **Customizable Interface**: Each task requires a different environment, and GIMP allows you to customize the view and behavior the way you like it. The widget theme allows you to change colors, widget spacings, and icon sizes, and there are custom tool sets in the toolbox. The interface is modulized into so-called docks, allowing you to stack them into tabs or keep them open in their own window. Pressing the *Tab* key will toggle them hidden. GIMP features a great *fullscreen mode* that allows you to not only preview your artwork but also to do editing work while using the most of your screen estate.

- **Photo Enhancement**: Numerous digital photo imperfections can be easily compensated for via GIMP. Fix *perspective distortion* caused by lens tilt simply by choosing the *corrective mode* in the transform tools. Eliminate lens *barrel distortion* and *vignetting* with a powerful filter but a simple interface. The included *channel mixer* gives you the flexibility and power to get your B/W photography to stand out the way you need.

- **Digital Retouching**: GIMP is ideal for advanced photo retouching techniques. Get rid of unneeded details using the *Clone* tool, or touch up minor details easily with the new *Healing* tool. With the *Perspective Clone* tool, it's not difficult to clone objects with perspective in mind just as easily as with the *Orthogonal* clone.

- **Hardware Support**: GIMP includes very unique support for various input devices out of the box, including pressure and tilt sensitive tablets, and a wide range of USB or MIDI controllers. You can bind often-used actions to device events such as rotating a USB wheel or moving a MIDI controller's slider. Change the size, angle, or opacity of a brush while you paint, or bind your favorite scripts to buttons. Speed up your workflow!

- **File Formats**: The file format support ranges from the common likes of JPEG (JFIF), GIF, PNG, and TIFF to special-use formats such as the multi-resolution and multi-color-depth Windows icon files. The architecture allows you to extend GIMP's format capabilities with a plug-in. You can find some rare format support in the GIMP plug-in registry. Thanks to the transparent virtual file system, it is possible to load and save files to and from remote locations using protocols such as FTP, HTTP, or even SMB (MS Windows shares) and SFTP/SSH. To save disk space, any format can be saved with an archive extension such as ZIP, GZ, or BZ2, and GIMP will transparently compress the file without you needing to do any extra steps.

Editing Capabilities

GIMP can handle just about any kind of image editing task, from minor retouching to major image editing. GIMP has an extensive toolset, including the ones you'd expect to find, such as the *Clone Stamp* tool. It also includes a *Healing* tool, which is very helpful for touching up blemishes, lines, creases, and other flaws in portraits (Figure 4-15). GIMP can support the CMYK color model (the Separate + plug-in must be installed, however).

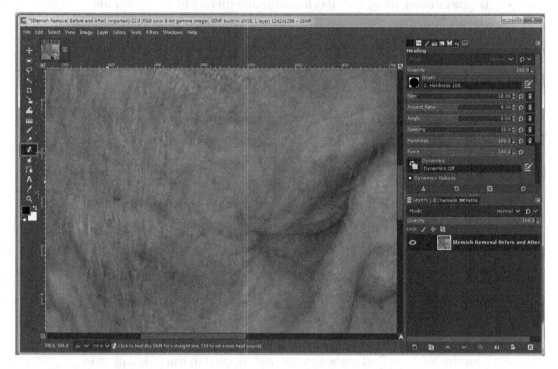

Figure 4-15. *The Healing tool is useful for removing blemishes and other imperfections in portraits*

The *Perspective* tool is handy for correcting images with lens distortion or correcting the perspective of buildings or other structures.

The image of this old church had a slant in it, but using the Perspective tool helps correct it (Figure 4-16).

Figure 4-16. *The Perspective tool corrects the slanted look of the image*

Graphics Creation

GIMP is a very capable tool for creating raster-based graphics from the ground up. It hosts a wide assortment of brush styles, effects, and other functions to create impressive designs. Figure 4-17 is an example of a design that was created entirely in GIMP.

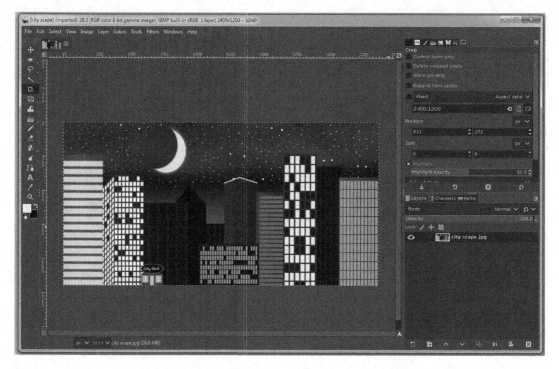

Figure 4-17. *A graphic design that was created entirely using GIMP*

GIMP Support

GIMP is a complex image editing program. Beginners who first jump into using it right away can be overwhelmed with the wide array of functions and features. A great starting point (aside from becoming familiar with the *User Manual* in the *Documentation* section of the website) is visiting the tutorial section. There are tutorials for beginning, intermediate, and expert users: `www.gimp.org/tutorials/`.

YouTube is also an excellent resource for learning GIMP. There are many video tutorials posted that will help the beginner come to grips with this powerful program. There are also a number of books about GIMP. Two great beginner's guides are *GIMP for Absolute Beginners* by Jan Smith with Roman Joost and my previous book, *Beginning Photo Retouching and Restoration Using GIMP* (both published by Apress).

Pixlr: Web-Based and Mobile Device Photo Editing

Pixlr is a family of web-based editors that work in your computer's web browser or on mobile devices. Each one is designed for a specialized area. There are three applications we'll look at: Pixlr X (quick and easy design), Pixlr E (advanced photo editor), and Photomash Studio (one-click visual creator).

Unlocking all of the features requires a monthly subscription to Pixlr Premium ($4.90 per month), but there's still plenty of functionality in the free versions of these programs.

- **Alternative to**: Adobe Photoshop, Photoshop Elements

- **Website**: www.pixlr.com

- **License**: Proprietary Freeware

- **Current Version**: Pixlr X, Pixlr E, Photomash Studio

- **Operating Systems**: Cross-platform (used in web browser or mobile devices)

- **Potential Savings**: $20.99 per month (Photoshop subscription)

The Pixlr tools are web-based and can be used in your browser or on your phone (Figure 4-18).

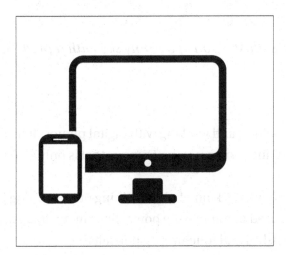

Figure 4-18. *The Pixlr tools can be used in your browser or on your phone*

Pixlr X

Pixlr X is for creating designs, using basic drawing tools, predesigned shapes, and elements. It offers options for creating new files in preset dimensions for a photo, social media, the Web, print, and video. In the example (Figure 4-19), the sunny sky illustration was created by using a blue background and the sun and clouds painted in. The predesigned border was then added.

Figure 4-19. *A digital illustration of a sunny sky with a predesigned border added*

Pixlr E

Pixlr E is primarily for editing and working with digital photos. It has most of the same tools found in other editing programs (the *Disperse* tool is only available in the Premium version).

It can handle just about any kind of photo editing or retouching job. In Figure 4-20, the *Clone* tool is being used to remove the power lines in the image. There's also a *Heal* tool for removing blemishes and touching up portraits.

Figure 4-20. *The Clone tool in Pixlr E being used to remove the power lines in this image*

Photomash Studio

This module of Pixlr is essentially a one-click solution for creating stylized visual assets for social media and marketing. Figure 4-21 shows the original photo on the left—when the image is opened in Photomash Studio, the background is automatically removed. The example in the center is a *Simple* profile background, and the far right is a *Trendy* profile background.

Figure 4-21. *The original image, a Simple profile, and Trendy profile*

There are stylized backgrounds that can be used to promote products on social media platforms (Figure 4-22) or YouTube. There are quite a few available in the free version, but to access all of them requires the paid version.

Figure 4-22. *Photomash Studio helps you promote your products on social media platforms*

Pixlr Support

There's a lot of help available under the *Help* menu; you'll have access to Pixlr User Community forums on Reddit, Instagram, Facebook, as well as YouTube tutorials.

If you're a new user, I'd recommend starting with the YouTube videos to get well acquainted with the Pixlr products.

Darktable: An Open Source Photography Workflow Program

Darktable is a free, open source for managing your photography workflow and working with RAW images.

Darktable is free, open source software and can be installed on as many computers as needed (Figure 4-23).

Figure 4-23. *Darktable can be installed on as many computers as needed*

Here are a few facts about Darktable at a glance:

- **Alternative to**: Adobe Lightroom
- **Website**: www.darktable.org/
- **License**: GPL
- **Current Version**: 3.8.1
- **Operating Systems**: Windows, Mac OX, Linux
- **Potential Savings**: $9.99 per month (Adobe Lightroom subscription)

Feature Highlights

Darktable supports a wide variety of digital cameras and offers a number of features that allow the processing of raw images. Here are the general features as listed on the Darktable website:

- **Nondestructive** editing throughout the complete workflow; your original images are never modified.

- **Take advantage of the real power of raw**: All Darktable core functions operate on **4x32-bit floating point pixel buffers**, enabling SSE instructions for speedups.

- **GPU accelerated image processing**: Many image operations are lightning fast, thanks to **OpenCL** support (runtime detection and enabling).

- **Professional color management**: Darktable is fully color managed, supporting automatic display profile detection on most systems, including built-in ICC profile support for sRGB, Adobe RGB, XYZ, and linear RGB color spaces.

- **Cross platform**: Darktable runs on Linux, macOS X/macports, BSD, Windows, and Solaris 11/GNOME.

- **Filtering and sorting**: Search your image collections by tags, image rating (stars), color labels, and many more, and use flexible database queries on all metadata of your images.

- **Image formats**: Darktable can import a variety of standard, raw, and high dynamic range image formats (e.g., JPEG, CR2, NEF, HDR, PFM, RAF, etc.).

- **Zero-latency, zoomable user interface**: Through multilevel software caches, Darktable provides a fluid experience.

- **Tethered shooting**: Support for instrumentation of your camera with live view for some camera brands.

- **Speaks your language**: Darktable currently comes with **21 translations**—Albanian, Catalan, Czech, Danish, Dutch, French, German, Greek, Hebrew, Hungarian, Italian, Japanese, Polish,

Portuguese (Brazilian and Portuguese), Russian, Slovak, Slovenian, Spanish, Swedish, and Ukrainian.

- **Powerful export system** supports Piwigo web albums, disk storage, 1:1 copy, and email attachments and can generate a simple HTML-based web gallery. Darktable allows you to export to low dynamic range (JPEG, PNG, TIFF), 16-bit (PPM, TIFF), or linear high dynamic range (PFM, EXR) images.

- **Never lose your image development settings:** Darktable uses both **XMP sidecar** files and its **fast database** for saving metadata and processing settings. All Exif data is read and written using libexiv2.

- **Automate repetitive tasks**: Many aspects of Darktable can be scripted in Lua.

RAW images are largely uncompressed, "pure" image data. RAW images are also known as digital negatives. Darktable allows nondestructive editing of your RAW images. Figure 4-24 shows the tone curve being adjusted in a RAW image.

Figure 4-24. *Adjusting the tone curve in a RAW image*

In the *Lightable* mode, your imported photos are displayed as thumbnail images (Figure 4-25).

Figure 4-25. *The Lighttable mode displays your imported photos as thumbnail images*

Darktable Support

Most of the information you need about Darktable can be found by clicking the *Resources* tab on the website. You'll have access to the FAQ page, the *User Manual,* and links to several video tutorials.

FotoSketcher: Automatically Turn Photos into Digital Art

FotoSketcher is an easy-to-use program for the Windows platform that gives your photos an artistic look in just a few clicks of the mouse. You don't need much image editing knowledge; just open the image and apply the filter style you want. I've been using it for several years, and it comes in very handy for my work from time to time.

Here are a few facts about FotoSketcher at a glance:

- **Alternative to:** Corel Painter Essentials 8

- **Website:** www.fotosketcher.com

- **License:** Proprietary Freeware

- **Current Version:** 3.8.0

- **Operating Systems:** Windows

- **Potential Savings:** $49.99

FotoSketcher offers a variety of artistic filter styles such as oil painting, color pencils, watercolors, etc. Figure 4-26 shows a close-up of an oil painting style being applied to an image.

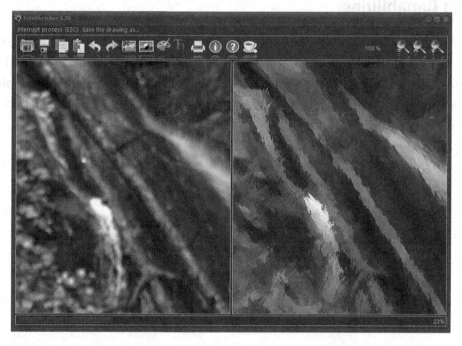

Figure 4-26. *Close-up view of an oil paint filter being applied to an image (Used with permission © David Thoiron 2015)*

Feature Highlights

Rather than performing a wide range of functions, FotoSketcher's primary purpose is converting photographic images into various types of digital art, so the list of highlights is rather short. Here's how they read on the software provider's website:

- 100% free

- More than 25 effects

- No artistic skill needed

- Over 6 million downloads

- Available in 23 different languages

Editing Capabilities

FotoSketcher has a rudimentary editor to adjust certain aspects of the source image, such as luminosity (brightness), contrast, saturation, blur/sharpen, and median filter (Figure 4-27). After adjusting the source image the way you want, the program applies the filter you choose to create the desired outcome on a new target image, which you can save in the JPEG, PNG, or BMP format (the source image reverts to its original state after closing the program).

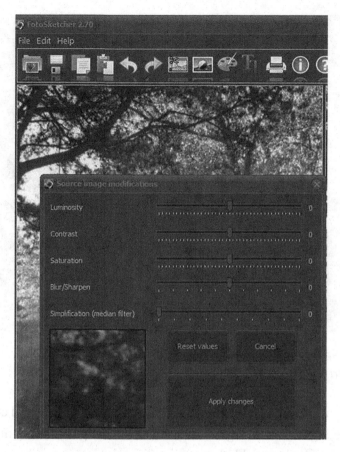

Figure 4-27.   *Close-up view of an oil paint filter being applied to an image (Used with permission © David Thoiron 2015)*

The parameters of each artistic filter can be fine-tuned, and the results appear in the preview window (Figure 4-28). You'll be able to add a canvaslike texture, soften the image edges, and add a frame if you like. After applying the *Draw* command, you can undo the command to reset the image if you don't like the results.

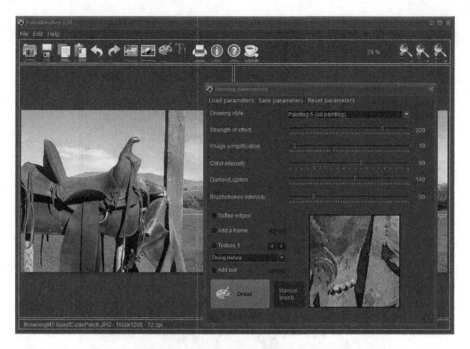

Figure 4-28. *The parameters of each artistic filter can be fine-tuned. (Used with permission © David Thoiron 2015)*

FotoSketcher also has a text editor, which can be used to create and customize images for marketing materials. Figure 4-29 shows the image of the saddle with the *Vintage* filter applied and text added.

Figure 4-29. *FotoSketcher includes a Text editor. (Used with permission © David Thoiron 2015)*

FotoSketcher Support

This program is really easy to use. However, you'll probably need to spend a little time experimenting with the filter parameters to achieve the results you want. The *Help* section of the website consists of two instructional videos (and there are numerous tutorials on YouTube as well).

Note   FotoSketcher should not be confused with PhotoSketcher, a paid macOS application. Although they are similar, the latter specializes in turning photos into digital pencil sketches. Along with FotoSketcher, there are several video tutorials about PhotoSketcher on YouTube, so it's a good idea to pay attention to the spelling when using the keyword search box.

Summary

In this chapter, you looked at some useful free and open source solutions for photo editing. PhotoScape is an easy-to-use editor with plenty of features. Paint.NET is a step up in functionality, reminiscent of Photoshop but far less complex. GIMP is arguably the most powerful and full-featured open source image editing program, and it is used by enthusiasts and professionals worldwide. The Pixlr family of web-based and mobile device solutions for editing images and adding effects offers ease and convenience. Darktable is an open source utility for reading, organizing, and working with RAW digital images. FotoSketcher is a great tool for converting digital photos into various types of art.

CHAPTER 5

Audio-Video Capture, Conversion, and Editing Software

The prevalence of video hosting sites such as YouTube affords the opportunity for small businesses to get their message out in a way not possible in the not-too-distant past. It's possible to digitize your old radio commercials from cassette tapes or make your own commercials, tutorials, or slideshows for posting on the Web. For the business owner who is a novice when it comes to working with audio and video, there are some no-cost options for capturing, converting, and editing audio and video files.

Here's a quick look at the software programs covered in this chapter:

- **fre:ac (Free Audio Converter)**: An open source program for ripping audio files from compact discs and converting WAV files into compressed audio files

- **Audacity**: An easy-to-use yet powerful open source audio editing tool for capturing and editing audio files

- **MPEG Streamclip**: A handy freeware tool for video format conversion

- **VirtualDub**: A free open source video capture and processing tool for Windows

- **OpenShot**: A simple, powerful free video editor

- **Kdenlive**: A powerful open source video editor for Linux and macOS

© Phillip Whitt 2022

P. Whitt, *Pro Freeware and Open Source Solutions for Business*, https://doi.org/10.1007/978-1-4842-8841-2_5

fre:ac (Free Audio Converter): An Open Source Audio CD Ripping Program

fre:ac is a handy, lightweight program for extracting the audio files from compact discs so they can be archived on your computer. It's primarily used for backing up files from music CDs, but it certainly has potential business applications such as archiving files from company training CDs, orientation CDs, etc.

Here are a few facts about fre:ac at a glance:

- **Alternative to**: illustrate dBpoweramp CD Ripper

- **Website**: www.freac.org

- **License**: GPL

- **Current Version**: 1.1.6

- **Operating Systems**: Windows, macOS X, Linux, and FreeBSD

- **Potential Savings**: $39.00 (single user)

Note   It's important to make sure you are working within the law when using this type of software. For example, if you own a business and are the legal copyright owner of the contents of an old training CD that was produced years earlier, then you are within your rights to copy and distribute the contents. If someone else owns the rights, then you need to obtain written permission to copy and use those files. When in doubt, check with your attorney.

---

fre:ac is available under the terms of the GPL and can be installed on as many computers as needed (Figure 5-1).

Figure 5-1. *fre:ac can be installed on as many computers as needed*

Upon launching the program, a *Tip of the day* window pops up (Figure 5-2). You can disable it if you wish, but it's a good idea to read the tips to help familiarize yourself with the functions and features that fre:ac offers.

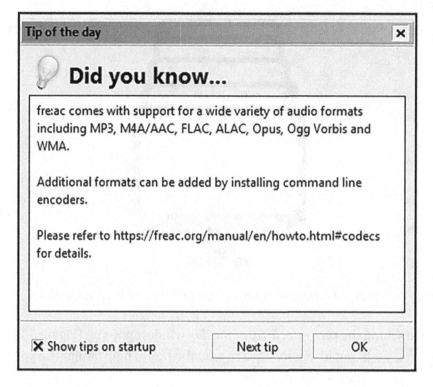

Figure 5-2. *The Tip of the day window displays upon launching fre:ac*

Feature Highlights

This program is a lightweight application with the primary functions of ripping files from CDs and converting audio files. Here's a rundown of its features as listed on the fre:ac website:

- Converter for MP3, MP4/M4A, WMA, Ogg Vorbis, FLAC, AAC, WAV, and Bonk formats

- Integrated CD ripper with CDDB/freedb title database support

- Portable application, so you can install on a USB stick and take it with you

- Multicore optimized encoders to speed up conversions on modern PCs

- Full Unicode support for tags and file names

- Easy to learn and use and still offers expert options when you need them

- Multilingual user interface available in 40 languages

- Completely free and open source without a catch

Figure 5-3 shows the workspace, displaying the files of royalty-free production music contained on a CD. By default, all of the tracks are selected but you can deselect the boxes of the files you don't want to rip.

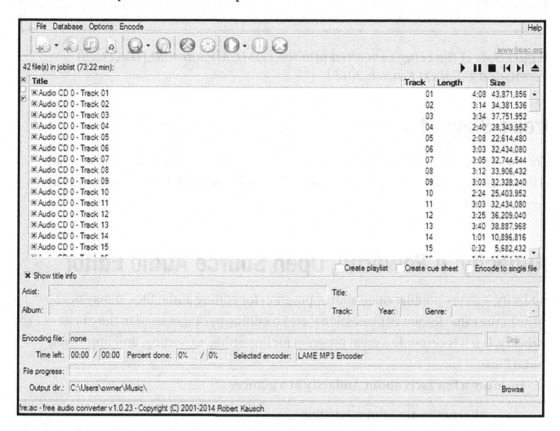

Figure 5-3. *You can rip all of the files from a CD at once or deselect the ones you don't need. (Used with permission © Robert Kausch 2015)*

Audio files can be converted from one format into another. There are spaces to add information such as the artist, track title, album, and music genre. Figure 5-4 shows the progress of converting a file into a LAME MP3 file. LAME refers to a free software codec used to compress audio into the lossy MP3 format.

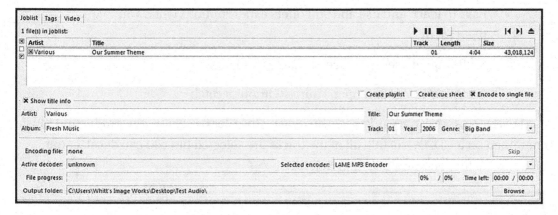

Figure 5-4. *A file being converted into the LAME MP3 format (Used with permission © Robert Kausch 2015)*

fre:ac Support

There is a *fre:ac User Guide* that can be accessed from the *Help* menu of the program (Help ➤ Help Topics). You can also read through the *Blog* and *Forums*, as well as a few YouTube videos.

Audacity: A Powerful, Open Source Audio Editor

Audacity is a very popular open source program for editing audio files. It may not be quite in the same league as professional audio editing packages used in the music industry, but it is certainly a great program for importing, exporting, and improving audio files.

Here are a few facts about Audacity at a glance:

- **Alternative to:** Adobe Audition

- **Website:** http://web.audacityteam.org

- **License:** GPL

- **Current Version:**

- **Operating Systems:** Windows, macOS, Linux

- **Potential Savings:** $39.99 per month

Audacity is an easy-to-use multitrack editor. It's available for use on Windows, macOS, and Linux, making it a widely used program by enthusiasts and pros on a budget.

Audacity software is copyright © 1999–2021 Audacity Team.

The name Audacity is a registered trademark.

Audacity is available under the terms of the GPL and can be installed on as many computers as needed (Figure 5-5).

Figure 5-5. *Audacity can be installed on as many computers as needed*

Feature Highlights

To see the long list of Audacity's features, click the *Features* tab on the website (`http://web.audacityteam.org/about/features`). The following is a quick rundown of several features as described on the website:

- Record live audio

- Record computer playback on any Windows Vista or later machine

- Convert tapes and records into digital recordings or CDs

- Edit WAV, AIFF, FLAC, MP2, MP3, or Ogg Vorbis sound files

- AC3, M4A/M4R (AAC), WMA, and other formats supported using optional libraries

- Cut, copy, splice, or mix sounds together

- Numerous effects including changing the speed or pitch of a recording

Audacity is primarily a tool used for music production. However, it has other practical applications beneficial to the business owner. Some businesses recycle advertisements from years past. If the advertisement is generic enough, it's possible to use it indefinitely. Audacity is a great tool to digitize radio spots that are stored on old audio cassettes (Figure 5-6). The audio files can be incorporated with video or still images, posted on your company website, Facebook, YouTube, or any number of sites to further extend the advertisement's usefulness.

Figure 5-6. *Audacity can digitize old radio ad spots for reuse*

Of course, it's also great for archiving your old personal music collection and childhood audio recordings.

Note   If you plan to repurpose old radio spots, it's best to make sure you own the rights to those spots. If it is unclear, obtain (written, if possible) permission from the manager of the station that produced and broadcasted them. When in doubt, check with an attorney.

Audacity can record audio by connecting one end of a patch cord to the line-in jack of your computer and the other to a playback device (such as a cassette player). Figure 5-7 shows the record button used to capture audio once the playback equipment is connected.

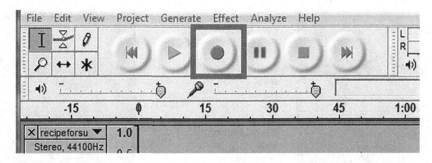

Figure 5-7. *Audacity's Record button for recording audio from playback devices (Used with permission © The Audacity Team 2015)*

Editing Capabilities

With Audacity, you can perform a number of editing tasks, such as importing audio, trimming away unwanted portions, and applying filters to modify or clean up the sound. There are many audio filters available for a wide range of purposes (Figure 5-8).

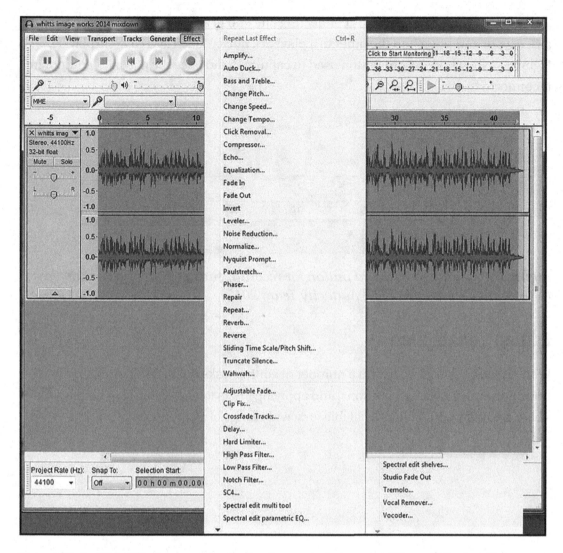

Figure 5-8.   *The Effects menu in Audacity contains many filters. (Used with permission © The Audacity Team 2015)*

Note   Audacity does not import or rip files from compact discs. Also, Audacity does not directly support MP3 conversion, and an additional library must be installed to export MP3 files.

Mono tracks can be split into stereo tracks. Although it's not true stereo, the file will exist on a left and right channel, each of which can be independently edited. Conversely, stereo tracks can be merged into a single track and can be output as mono.

Audacity can also generate click tracks, which are audio cues to aid in timing in recording music. Click tracks are also used as a means of synchronizing audio to moving images (Figure 5-9).

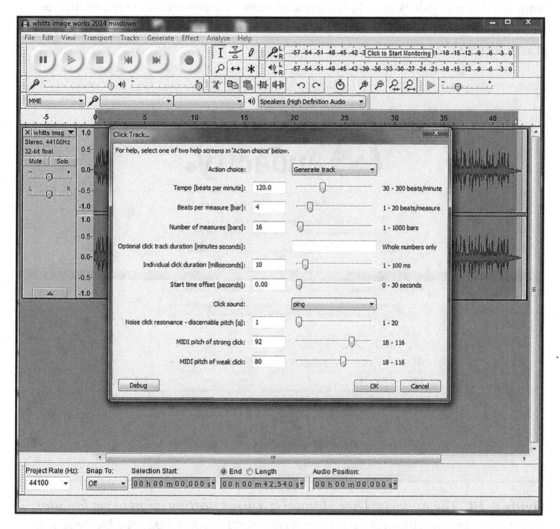

Figure 5-9. *Audacity's Click Track dialog offers many options. (Used with permission © The Audacity Team 2015)*

Audacity Support

Audacity is a popular program, so there's plenty of help available. The *User Manual* on the Audacity website (`http://manual.audacityteam.org/o/quick_help.html`) is the best starting point to familiarize yourself with the basics (Figure 5-10). There are beginning tutorials, and the FAQ page provides a lot of information. YouTube has numerous tutorial videos as well, but some of them may be for older versions. Up-to-date tutorials can be found here: `http://wiki.audacityteam.org/wiki/Category:Tuto rial#external`.

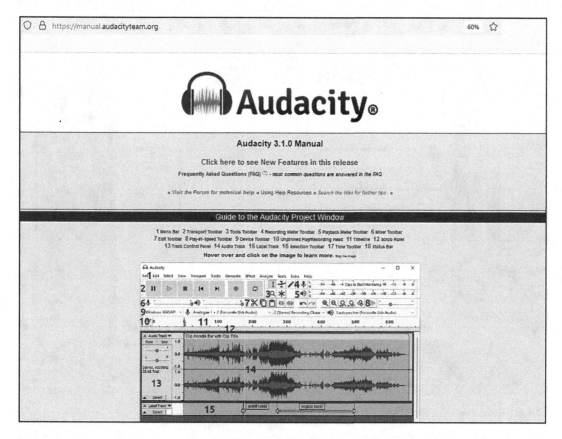

Figure 5-10. *The Audacity User Manual is a great starting point to get familiar with this program (Audacity software is copyright © 1999–2021 Audacity Team. The name Audacity is a registered trademark)*

MPEG Streamclip: A Handy, Free Video Conversion Tool

MPEG Streamclip is a useful, lightweight program primarily for converting standard definition video files from one format into another. It also offers some rudimentary editing features. One of this program's uses is converting larger video files (such as AVI) into formats suitable for playback on mobile devices.

Here are a few facts about MPEG Streamclip at a glance:

- **Alternative to:** AVS Video Converter

- **Website:** www.squared5.com

- **License:** Proprietary Freeware

- **Current Version:** 1.2

- **Operating Systems:** Windows, macOS

- **Potential Savings:** $49 (annual subscription to AVS4You.com)

It should be mentioned that there is one caveat that accompanies the use of MPEG Streamclip; it requires that QuickTime Alternative is installed on your computer. This, however, isn't a huge obstacle. QuickTime Alternative can be downloaded (for free) from the following link on Codecs.com: www.free-codecs.com/download/quicktime_alternative.htm.

Feature Highlights

MPEG Streamclip's features are listed in detail on the Squared 5 website. Here is the abridged version (and reformatted into a bullet list) of this program's features from the website:

- Play and edit file formats such as QuickTime, DV, AVI, MPEG-4, MPEG-1, MPEG-2, or VOB.

- Transport streams with MPEG, PCM, or AC3 audio to QuickTime, DV, AVI/DivX, and MPEG-4 with high-quality encoding and even uncompressed or HD video.

- Video conversion is performed in the YUV color space.

- Other optional video processing features include a powerful motion-adaptive deinterlacer, a field dominance converter, a chroma reinterlacer, and an option to perform interlaced scaling instead of progressive scaling.

- Audio can be converted to uncompressed or to IMA, AAC, MP2, or AMR using the high-quality MP1/MP2/AC3/PCM built-in decoders of MPEG Streamclip; it is also kept in perfect sync with video using a timekeeping system.

- Save edited movies as MOV files and (when possible) as AVI or MP4 files. Edited MPEG-1 or MPEG-2 files are saved as MPEG or TS files.

- Convert MPEG-2 transport streams into muxed MPEG-2 files for immediate burning at full quality with most DVD authoring applications.

- Handle files and streams larger than 4 GB, split in any number of segments, or with multiple audio tracks, and can also optionally handle timecode breaks. It is compatible with MPEG-1 and MPEG-2 video, MPEG layer 1/2 (MP1/MP2) audio, AC3/A52 audio, and PCM audio.

- The player lets you preview the files and transport streams before doing the conversion; it also lets you visually set the In and Out points for the conversion so you can convert just the part of the file you are interested in.

Once QuickTime Alternative is installed, upon launching MPEG Streamclip, the workspace window appears with the Squared 5 logo in the center (a square with five small circles).

For file conversions, it's essentially a matter of choosing the output format you want. There is a menu with choices of frame size, compression quality, and other options depending on the format chosen. MPEG Streamclip can come in handy for converting larger video formats into MPEG-4 files, commonly used on mobile devices (Figure 5-11).

Figure 5-11. *Larger video formats can be converted to MPEG-4, which is used on mobile devices*

Editing Capabilities

MPEG Streamclip offers only limited editing functions. It is possible to set In and Out points so that only the desired portions of the movie are converted to the new file. There is an *Adjustments* dialog box for adjusting the brightness, contrast, saturation (Figure 5-12), and volume of the movie. There is also an option to add basic text as a watermark that appears in the lower right hand corner of the video frame.

Figure 5-12. *Brightness is improved using the Adjustments dialog box*

MPEG Streamclip Support

There's no real documentation on the Squared 5 website to speak of (other than the *Features* page and the website itself).

Fortunately, YouTube has a few instructional videos, many of which are introductory tutorials. MPEG Streamclip is a simple enough program to ensure that most users will learn it quickly.

VirtualDub: Open Source Video Processing for Windows

VirtualDub is a video capturing program that can be used on 32 and 64 bit Windows platforms. If you're still using an older version of Windows, this could be a good option.

Here are a few facts about VirtualDub at a glance:

- **Alternative to:** Adobe Premier Elements

- **Website:** www.virtualdub.org

- **License:** GPL

- **Current Version:** 1.10.4

- **Operating Systems:** Windows

- **Potential Savings:** $99.99

VirtualDub is available under the terms of the GPL and can be installed on as many computers as needed (Figure 5-13).

Figure 5-13. *VirtualDub can be installed on as many computers as needed*

VirtualDub is really more of a video capture and processing tool than it is a general purpose video editor. Among its strengths are filters such as *Levels, Hue/Saturation/Value,* and many others. VirtualDub can make color enhancements and improve exposure in less-than-perfect video clips (Figure 5-14).

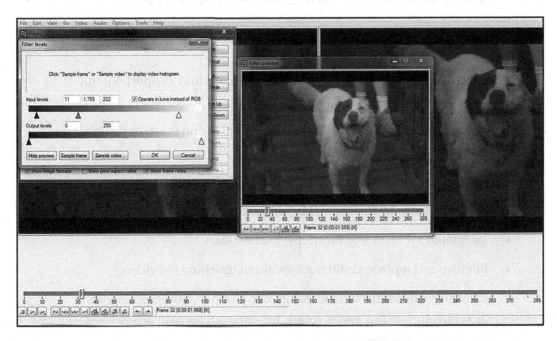

Figure 5-14. *Improving a dark video using the Levels filter within VirtualDub*

Note   It's helpful to have a video capture card or device that captures video as AVI files to your computer. Otherwise, you can use a free program like MPEG Streamclip (also covered in this chapter) to convert other formats to an AVI file in order to use VirtualDub.

Feature Highlights

VirtualDub has an extensive list of features primarily for managing AVI files. I've listed them here as they are shown on the website, although a couple of them are slightly abridged:

- Fractional frame rates

- Optimized disk access for more consistent hard disk usage

- Create AVI2 (OpenDML) files to break the AVI 2GB barrier and multiple files to break the FAT32 4GB limit

- Integrated volume meter and histogram for input-level monitoring

- Real-time downsizing, noise reduction, and field swapping

- Verbose monitoring, including compression levels, CPU usage, and free disk space

- Access hidden video formats your capture card may support but not have a setting for, such as 352x480

- Keyboard and mouse shortcuts for faster operation (such as just hit F6 to capture)

- Clean interface layout: caption, menu bar, info panel, status bar

- Read and write AVI2 (OpenDML) and multi-segment AVI clips.

- Integrated MPEG-1 and Motion-JPEG decoders

- Remove and replace audio tracks without touching the video

- Extensive video filter set, including blur, sharpen, emboss, smooth, 3x3 convolution, flip, resize rotate, brightness/contrast, levels, deinterlace, and threshold

- Bilinear and bicubic resampling so no blocky resizes or rotates here

- Decompress and recompress both audio and video

- Remove segments of a video clip and save the rest without recompressing

- Adjust frame rate, decimate frames, and 3:2 pulldown removal

- Preview the results with live audio

Editing Capabilities

VirtualDub is somewhat limited when compared to a more full-featured program. For example, video processed using this software requires a separate authoring program to write a DVD. Another limitation is the fact that it only handles Microsoft AVI files.

However, it does offer a generous filter set to improve video quality and to add a variety of effects. The preview window provides a side-by-side comparison of the original dark video (Figure 5-15).

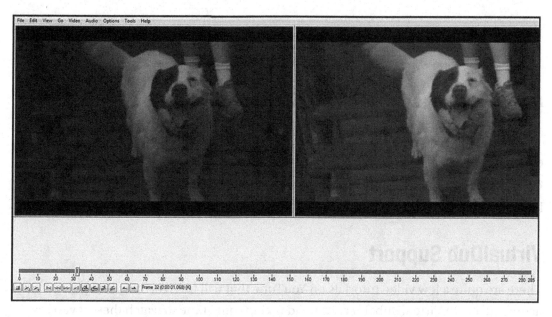

Figure 5-15. *Side-by-side comparison of original video and the clip with a filter applied*

VirtualDub also allows the placement of logos or images over a video clip. In Figure 5-16, I placed a simplified version of my logo over a sample clip of a film transfer done recently (I post sample clips on YouTube to help me promote my film conversion services). I created the logo using GIMP 2.8 and exported it in the PNG file format with a transparent background.

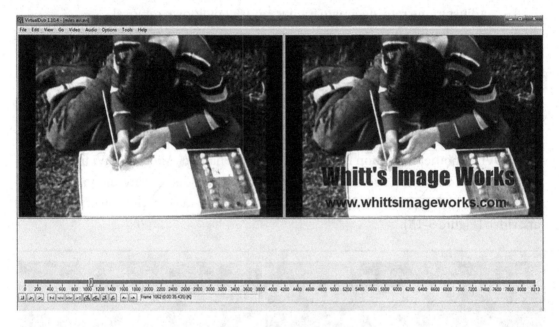

Figure 5-16. *A logo added to a video clip in VirtualDub*

VirtualDub also allows you to remove unwanted sections of video to create a new, edited clip by using the *Mark In* and *Mark Out* feature. You can also remove existing audio tracks and replace them with new ones if needed. After the video clip has been processed and edited, you can save it as a new AVI file.

VirtualDub Support

There are quite a few video tutorials on YouTube that will help the new user get acquainted with VirtualDub. I recommend taking some time to watch these if you are new to video editing. There is also a support forum on the official VirtualDub website.

OpenShot: A Versatile Free Video Editor

OpenShot is a nonlinear video editor that is easy to use yet powerful enough to create impressive videos.

Here are a few facts about OpenShot at a glance:

- **Alternative to:** Adobe Premier Elements

- **Website:** www.openshot.org

- **License:** GPL

- **Current Version:** 2.6.1

- **Operating Systems:** Windows, macOS, Linux

- **Potential Savings:** $99.99

OpenShot is available under the terms of the GPL, so it can be installed on as many computers as needed (Figure 5-17).

Figure 5-17. *OpenShot can be installed on as many computers as needed*

Here are the features of OpenShot as listed on the website:

- Cross-platform video editing software (Linux, Mac, and Windows)

- Support for many video, audio, and image formats

- Powerful curve-based key frame animations

- Desktop integration (drag and drop support)

- Unlimited tracks/layers

- Clip resizing, scaling, trimming, snapping, rotation, and cutting

- Video transitions with real-time previews

- Compositing, image overlays, watermarks

- Title templates, title creation, subtitles

- Three-dimensional animated titles (and effects)

- Advanced timeline (including drag and drop, scrolling, panning, zooming, and snapping)

- Frame accuracy (step through each frame of video)

- Time-mapping and speed changes on clips (slow/fast, forward/backward, etc.)

- Audio mixing and editing

- Digital video effects, including brightness, gamma, hue, grayscale, chroma key (blue screen/green screen), and many more

OpenShot is a useful, free open source video editing program available for Windows, macOS, and Linux. It has a simple, uncluttered interface. Figure 5-18 shows a video clip displayed in the *Preview* window.

Figure 5-18. *A video clip displayed in the Preview window*

OpenShot offers a variety of transitions that can be placed between video clips, still images, or a mix of both (Figure 5-19). There are a number of effects that can be added as well.

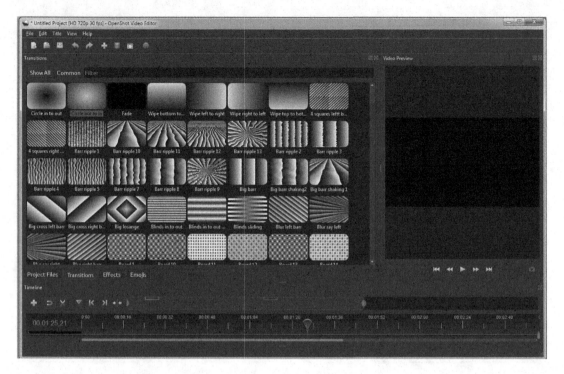

Figure 5-19. *OpenShot offers a number of transitions that can be placed between video clips, still images, or a mix of both*

By default, OpenShot displays the interface in the *Simple View* mode, but if you prefer it can be switched to the *Advanced View.* In addition to the features shown in the Simple View, the Properties, Effects menu, and Transitions menu are also displayed (Figure 5-20).

Figure 5-20. *The Advanced View mode*

When you're ready to export your project, the Export Video menu (Figure 5-21) allows you to *Select a Profile to start* (such as Blu-Ray/AVCHD, DVD, Device, or Web). You can also select the *Target* (such as MP4, MPEG 2, MOV, AVI, etc.), the *Video Profile* (such as DV, HD, etc.), and the Quality (low, medium, or high).

Figure 5-21. *The Export Video menu*

OpenShot Support

For those new to video editing, OpenShot might seem a bit daunting. The best place to start is to go to the *User Guide* found here: https://cdn.openshot.org/static/files/user-guide/index.html.

Because it is ostensibly one of the most popular open source video editors available, there are quite a few YouTube video tutorials to help you get up and running.

Kdenlive: Open Source Video Editing for Most Needs

Kdenlive is feature-rich, free, open source cross-platform video editor developed for everything from basic editing to professional work.

Here are a few facts about Kdenlive at a glance:

- **Alternative to**: Adobe Premier

- **Website**: www.kdenlive.org

- **License**: GPL

- **Current Version**: 22.04.3

- **Operating Systems**: Windows, BSD, Linux

- **Potential Savings**: $99.99

Kdenlive is available under the terms of the GPL, so it can be installed on as many computers as needed (Figure 5-22).

Figure 5-22. *Kdenlive can be installed on as many computers as needed*

Kdenlive is capable of producing basic video clips but is also powerful enough for professional quality work (although not on par with Adobe Premier). It supports DV, AVCHD, and HDV editing. Figure 5-23 shows a video clip in the timeline of Kdenlive.

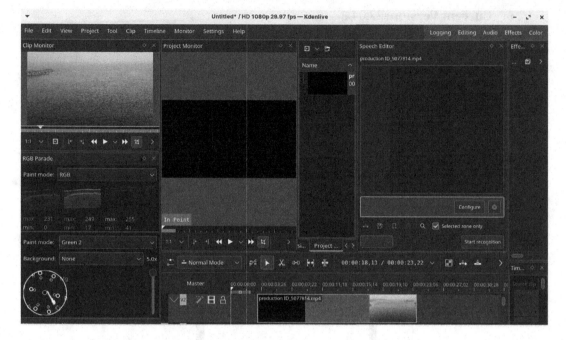

Figure 5-23. *A video clip in the Kdenlive timeline*

Feature Highlights

Kdenlive boasts functions for the creative filmmaker. The full list can be found on the *Features* page of the Kdenlive website. The following list is a condensed, quick overview of the features from the Kdenlive website:

- Multitrack video editing

- Use any audio/video format

- Configurable interface and shortcuts

- Titler

- Many effects and transitions

- Audio and video scopes

- Proxy editing

- Automatic backup

- Online resources

- Timeline preview

- Keyframable effects

- Themable interface

Editing Capabilities

Kdenlive offers some tools normally found in high-end video editing programs. There are tons of effects for working with audio, adjusting contrast, adding fun effects, etc. Figure 5-24 shows the Effect list in the far left panel; in the example, the *Saturation* dialog is active.

Figure 5-24. *There are many effects available in Kdenlive*

More often than not, the quality of the video shot with consumer camcorders and video cameras can stand improvement. There are a number of effects in Kdenlive to improve the quality of the footage.

The *Bezier Curves* dialog (Figure 5-25) helps fine-tune color and tone.

Figure 5-25. *The Bezier Curves dialog can help fine-tune color and tone*

When your movie is completed, there are several video format choices available for output. There are several options (Figure 5-26) for rendering it as Generic (HD for web or mobile devices), Ultra High Definition, Old TV Definition (DVD), and an experimental Hardware Accelerated.

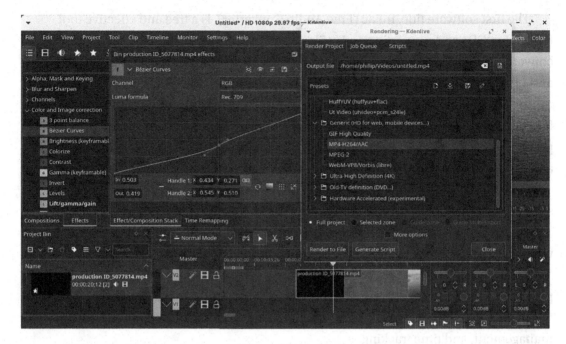

Figure 5-26. *Kdenlive offers numerous video formats for output of your movie*

Kdenlive Support

Kdenlive might be more overwhelming than OpenShot is, so I recommend becoming well acquainted with this program. The *Kdenlive/Manual* is the best place to start. It can be found by clicking the User Manual tab on the home page. Here is the link: `https://docs.kdenlive.org/en/`.

There are plenty of Kdenlive video tutorials on YouTube as well, everything from beginning tutorials to advanced editing techniques.

Summary

This chapter looked at several no-cost solutions for working with audio and video files. This can be especially useful for the small business looking to create marketing messages to get on to platforms like YouTube, social media, and other avenues where audio and video is effective.

The first software title, fre:ac (Free Audio Converter), is a free and effective tool for ripping CDs and converting audio files from one format to another. Audacity also converts audio files, but it also captures analog audio from sources such as audio tapes and LP records. Audacity offers effects filters and editing capabilities for audio.

MPEG Streamclip is a handy tool with rudimentary editing abilities primarily used for converting video files from one format to another. VirtualDub is a video capture and processing application for Windows. It offers a wealth of effects filters, including color and exposure correction.

OpenShot is a simple yet powerful free video editing program that offers an ample selection of transitions and effects to produce high-quality videos.

Kdenlive is a feature-rich video editing program capable of producing pro-quality work. It boasts a number of effects and transition styles. It can also edit HD video.

For additional no-cost programs, there are a couple of other audio and video programs as well as disc burning software listed in Appendix B of this book.

In the next chapter, you'll look at some free options for project planning, inventory management, and time tracking.

CHAPTER 6

Project Planning, Inventory Management, and Time-Tracking Software

Organization and accuracy are crucial in any business. During my early days in the retail hardware business, projects were planned on pen and paper. Inventory specialists did physical counts of the store's inventory twice a year (in those days, we were not computerized). Tracking the time invested in business activities was largely guesswork.

This chapter looks at several powerful, free options for planning projects and keeping track of inventory, human resources, and billable time. Here's a quick look at the software programs covered in this chapter:

Project Management

- **ProjectLibre**: An open source program that is compatible with but an alternative to Microsoft Project

- **Asana:** Free project management for up to 15 members

Human Resources Management

- **MintHCM:** Free, open source human capital management

© Phillip Whitt 2022
P. Whitt, *Pro Freeware and Open Source Solutions for Business*, https://doi.org/10.1007/978-1-4842-8841-2_6

Inventory Management

- **ABC Inventory**: A free, robust program for inventory management

Time Tracking

- **My Hours**: A free, web-based time-tracking solution ideal for solo freelancers or small teams

ProjectLibre: An Open Source Alternative to Microsoft Project

ProjectLibre is an extremely useful program for creating and managing company projects. It's capable of everything from simple projects requiring only a few tasks to complex projects involving multiple colleagues.

Here are a few facts about ProjectLibre at a glance:

- **Alternative to**: Microsoft Project

- **Website**: www.projectlibre.org

- **License**: CPAL (Common Public Attribution License)

- **Current Version**: 1.9.3

- **Operating Systems**: Cross-platform

- **Potential Savings**: $680.00

ProjectLibre is free and open source software offered under the terms of the CPAL (Common Public Attribution License) and can be installed on as many computers as needed (Figure 6-1).

Figure 6-1. *ProjectLibre can be installed on as many computers as needed*

ProjectLibre is described on the software provider's website as the open source replacement for Microsoft Project. With the non-collaborative, on premises version of MS project costing about $680.00, it's certainly worth trying out.

Note   According to the website, ProjectLibre is currently developing a cloud-based version for team solutions.

Feature Highlights

According to the website, ProjectLibre has been downloaded about 6,000,000 times in 193 countries. Here's a quick look at the features:

- Compatibility with Microsoft Project
- Gantt chart
- Network diagram
- Earned value costing
- Resource histograms

After downloading and installing ProjectLibre, you're ready to start a new project (Figure 6-2). The project can be given a name, the name of project manager, start date (it assigns the current date by default), and any relevant notes.

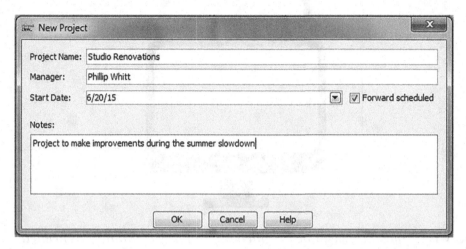

Figure 6-2. *Starting a new project in ProjectLibre (Used with permission © Marc O'Brien 2015)*

Adjustments can be made in the *Project Information* dialog box (Figure 6-3). Under the *General* tab are settings such as start and finish dates, status, the expense type, project type, etc.

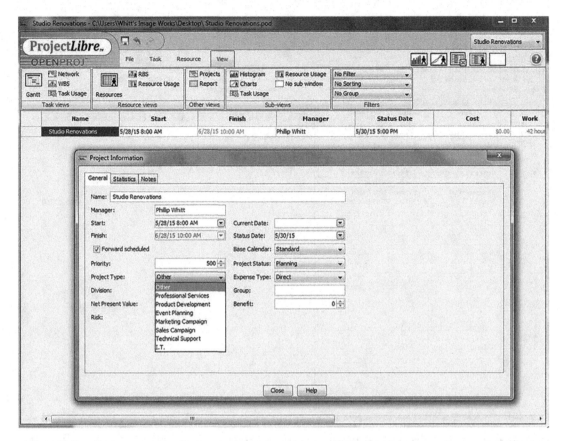

Figure 6-3. *The Project Information dialog box (Used with permission © Marc O'Brien 2015)*

The workspace shows the tasks of my project on the left as data in a spreadsheet and on the right graphically represented as a Gantt chart (Figure 6-4). A Gantt chart is essentially a bar chart that illustrates the start/finish dates of tasks in the project.

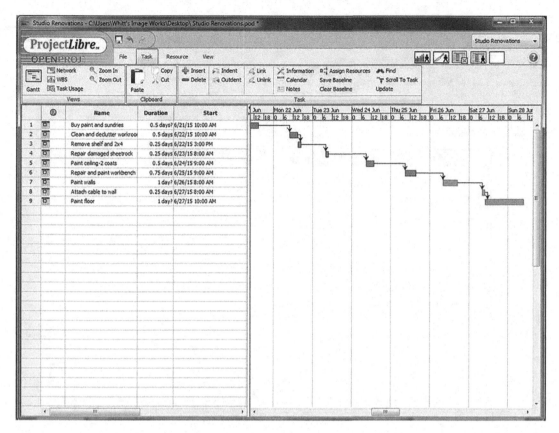

Figure 6-4. *The Gantt chart illustrates the start and finish dates of each task in the project. (Used with permission © Marc O'Brien 2015)*

Note   In my sample project, the arrows shown represent the order in which the tasks must be undertaken (known as dependencies). This basically means that a specific task must be completed before I can move on to the next one. The arrows are inserted by clicking a task on the Gantt chart and dragging a line to the sequential task in the workflow. When the mouse button is released, the arrow is created.

ProjectLibre Support

A great way to become familiar with ProjectLibre is to open the *Help* menu and cycle through the *Tip of the Day window* (Figure 6-5). *There is a Global User Group,* as well as several region-specific groups that offer updates, news events, and blogs to help keep users up to speed.

Figure 6-5. *Taking some time to cycle through and read each tip of the day will help you quickly become acquainted with ProjectLibre. (Used with permission ©️ Marc O'Brien 2015)*

There is an introductory video that can be viewed here: `https://youtu.be/9xwR4JCBaIU.`

There are also a number of YouTube tutorials that are very helpful in learning this program.

Asana: Free for individuals or small teams

Asana: Free Basic Project Management

If you're looking for a lightweight project manager for small teams, Asana offers a free plan that might fit the bill.

Here are a few facts about Asana at a glance:

- **Alternative to:** Smartsheet

- **Website:** `www.asana.com`

- **License:** Proprietary SAAS

- **Operating Systems**: Web-based/cross-platform

- **Potential Savings**: $7.00 per month

Asana is a web-based project management tool that offers a free plan for single users or for teams of up to 15 people. It can be synced across computers and mobile devices (Figure 6-6).

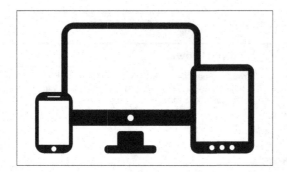

Figure 6-6. *Asana can be synced across multiple devices*

Feature Highlights

The free version of Asana offers a number of useful features, making it a worthy web-based application for project management. Here's a look at a few as listed on the website:

- Unlimited projects

- Unlimited messages

- Unlimited activity log

- Unlimited file storage (100MB per file)

- Collaborate with up to 15 teammates

- List view projects

- Board view projects

- Calendar view

- Assignee and due dates

- Project overview

- Project brief

- iOS and Android mobile apps

- Time tracking with integrations

- 100+ free integrations with your favorite apps

On the home page, you'll be greeting with the current date and the option of *My Priorities*, *Projects*, and *People* similar to that shown in Figure 6-7.

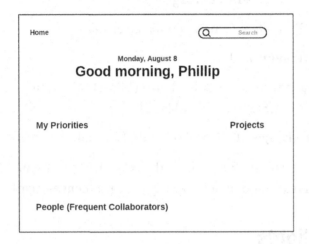

Figure 6-7. *Your Asana home page is similar to the one shown here*

The *My Tasks* page provides a list to add tasks (and milestones when important tasks are accomplished), and files (such as images or video clips) can be added to projects.

New projects can be created by selecting *Blank Project* (which starts from scratch), *Use a template* (choose from library), or importing a spreadsheet.

Asana Support

There are a lot of features to Asana, and although it offers a lot (even the free version), it might be a bit overwhelming at first. A great place to start is on Asana's YouTube channel: `https://www.youtube.com/c/asana`.

This channel shows mainly the new features in Asana, which will provide a broad view of how the program works. There are a number of other YouTube videos that can provide assistance and get you well acquainted with Asana.

MintHCM: Free, Open Source Human Capital Management

MintHCM is a free, open source solution for human resource operations.
   Here are a few facts about MintHCM at a glance:

- **Alternative to**: Zoho People

- **Website**: `https://minthcm.org/`

- **License**: GNU Affero General Public License

- **Current Version**: 3.1.1

- **Operating Systems**: Windows, Linux (MintHCM requirements are PHP 7.1 and MySQL 5.6-5.7 or MariaDB)

- **Potential Savings**: $1.25 per user/billed annually

MintHCM is offered under the terms of the GNU Affero General Public License. To learn more, you can read about it here: `www.gnu.org/licenses/agpl-3.0.en.html`.

Feature Highlights

MintHCM offers a wide range of features. These features (as listed on the website) are as follows:

- Recruitment—effortless coordination of talent acquisition procedures

- Job description—keeping the responsibilities and career paths transparent

- Employer branding—ensuring the positive image of the company as a worthy employer

- Onboarding—getting the new joiners on board

- Employee profile—handy catalog of essential personnel's information

- Competence and skills—a transparent overview of expertise and know-how in the organization

- Employment history—keeping a comprehensive catalog of employment contracts

- Employee performance—evaluating employee performance

- Time management—a way to efficiently manage daily tasks and perfect the work, on time

- Calendar—meeting deadlines, and not in a hurry

- Travel and expenses—delegating employees to work outside the headquarters

- Resources booking—exchanging the material assets within the company

- Leave management—keeping track of the absences and precisely distributing responsibilities

- Off boarding—letting people go without letting go of the know-how

- Workplace—keeping track of office space occupancy

- Analytics—taking advantage of the data collected in the system for the analytical purposes

- System administration—single-handedly assigning roles, giving users permissions, and setting up the system

You can try out an online demo of MintHCM without downloading anything to test it out. You'll need to submit your name and email address on the *Demo* page: https://minthcm.org/demo/. You'll then be sent a username and password to gain access to the online demo.

MintHCM Support

It's important to note that there are certain requirements for using MintHCM. To install MintHCM, you will need Linux or Windows platform, a web server with PHP installed, and a database (Figure 6-8).

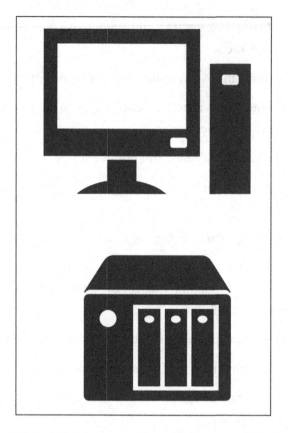

Figure 6-8. *To install MintHCM, you will need Linux or Windows platform, a web server with PHP installed, and a database*

The *Support* page (`https://minthcm.org/support/`) provides guidance on the installation, configuration, and use of MintHCM.

You can also subscribe to the MintHCM YouTube channel for additional information.

ABC (Always Better Control) Inventory: A Free Option for the Small- and Mid-Sized Business

ABC Inventory from Almyta Systems is a free subset of their commercial package. It might be just the solution for a budget-minded small warehouse or distribution center.

Here are a few facts about ABC Inventory at a glance:

- **Alternative to**: InFlow

- **Website**: www.almyta.com/abc_inventory_software.asp

- **License**: Proprietary Freeware

- **Current Version**: Not specified

- **Operating Systems**: Windows

- **Potential Savings**: $79.99 per month

ABC Inventory can be installed on as many workstations as you wish, but you won't be able to link them together to read and write the same information (an upgrade to the paid version is required). Of course, if managing inventory is handled from a single workstation, this won't be an issue.

Feature Highlights

ABC Inventory is a robust program. As you can see, it has a long list of features making it a worthy program to try:

- Single user (multiuser available in the commercial version only)

- Multiple companies

- Multiple warehouses for a company

- Multiple currencies/currency rates auto-update

- User-selectable decimal places for currency

- Multiple logos

- User-selectable decimal places for inventory units

- Password protection

- Screen and report permissions by user or group

- Screens and reports customizations

- Export data to Microsoft Excel, Word, HTML, and text functionality

- Copy to new company function/company backups

- Restore last function/restore any function

After installing ABC Inventory, it's a good idea to open the sample *XYZ, Corp. entry* to learn your way around the program, as it's rather complex. When you're ready, you can create a real company with clean data (Figure 6-9). To create a new test, choose *New Company with Test Data.* You can also link to an existing networked company.

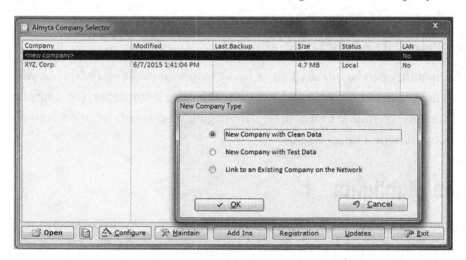

Figure 6-9. *The New Company Type option window (Used with permission ©️ Almyta Systems 2015)*

New items can be added to the Inventory Item Master List. Parameters such as category, package type, manufacturer/model, and other pertinent information can be input (Figure 6-10).

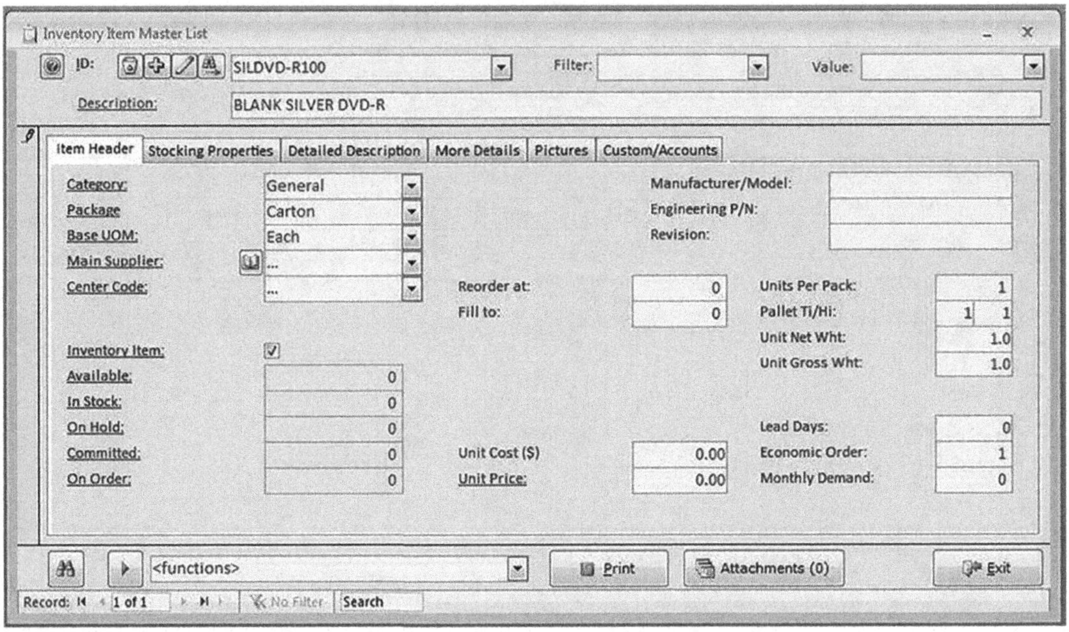

Figure 6-10. *Adding a new item to the Inventory Item Master List (Used with permission © Almyta Systems 2015)*

New items can be added to the Inventory Item Master List. Parameters such as category, package type, manufacturer/model, and other pertinent information can be input (Figure 6-11).

173

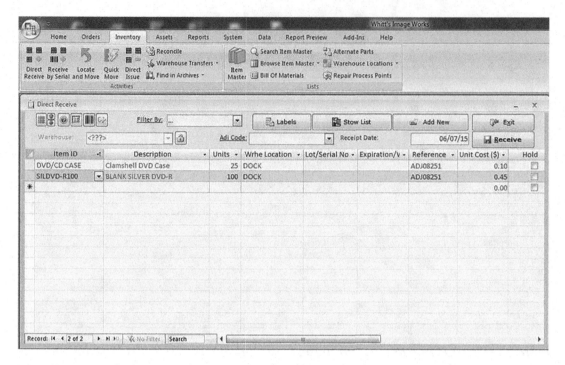

Figure 6-11. *The inventory master list (Used with permission © Almyta Systems 2015)*

ABC Inventory Support

The *Help* tab offers a tutorial on navigating through the menus (Figure 6-12). Although support is not offered for the free version of ABC Inventory, there are one or two video overviews on YouTube. The software documentation can be accessed from this URL: www.almyta.com/v3/.

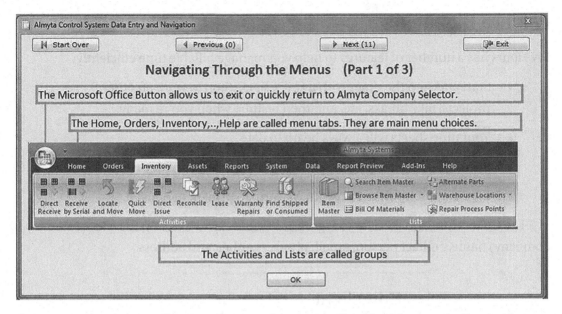

Figure 6-12. *A tutorial on navigating the menus (Used with permission © Almyta Systems 2015)*

My Hours: A Free, Web-Based Time-Tracking Tool for Individuals or Teams

The importance of keeping track of billable time spent working on client projects can't be understated. It's amazing how much billable time can be lost if it's not tracked correctly. My Hours is an easy-to-use, web-based program that any freelancer should try.

Here are a few facts about My Hours at a glance:

- **Alternative to**: Bill4Time

- **Website**: www.myhours.com

- **License**: Proprietary Freeware

- **Current Version**: Not specified

- **Operating Systems**: Web-based

- **Potential Savings**: $30.00 per month

My Hours is a time-tracking tool that is essential for managing billable hours. My Hours offers a free plan for single users or teams.

Feature Highlights

My Hours has a number of features to help you manage billable time efficiently:

- Start and stop the timer with a single click. Stop to work on other projects, take breaks, etc. and then resume when you're ready.

- Your time sheets will always be up to date.

- Set up your clients, projects, tasks, and hourly rates with ease.

- Export your report to Excel or CSV format, print it, or email it.

The Clients function (similar to Figure 6-13) allows you to set up the client (or company) name, contact person, email, phone number, and address.

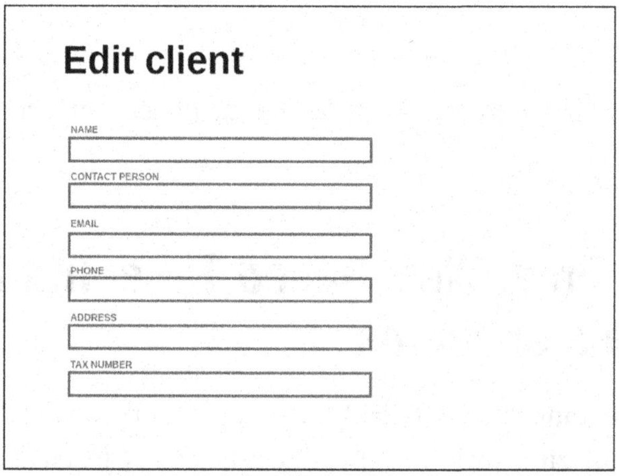

Edit client

NAME

CONTACT PERSON

EMAIL

PHONE

ADDRESS

TAX NUMBER

Figure 6-13. *You can easily set up new clients in My Hours*

The Manage Project function allows you to set up the name of the project, the client's name, indicate if the project is billable, the hourly rate, and any additional notes (Figure 6-14). The time log of each project can be edited, such as setting the duration of the project.

Manage Project

NAME	Restore Photo With Heavy Damage
CLIENT	Bright Images

☑ THIS PROJECT IS BILLABLE

INVOICE METHOD	Project hourly rate
PROJECT RATE	$ 25
NOTES	Make sure all damage is repaired and photo colorized

Figure 6-14. *Setting up a new project (Used with permission © My Hours (Spica International) 2015)*

To track the time in your projects, add a time log, which looks similar to the one shown in Figure 6-15. You'll be able to add a project name, task, and tags. You can also record the start and finish times, the project duration, and billable hours.

Track

TODAY Monday August 8, 2022   Compact | Expand

Add time log

PROJECT	TASK	TAGS

START	FINISH	DURATION

Figure 6-15. *Track the start/finish times, project duration, and billable hours*

The *Activity Chart* similar to the graphic shown in Figure 6-16 displays how many billable hours were logged in a given time frame. This helps expose any irregularities and when the busiest times are. Utilizing this feature will help you use your time more efficiently.

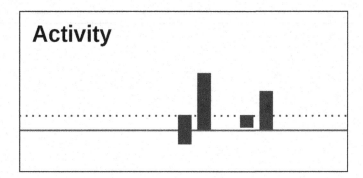

Figure 6-16. *My Hours can display an Activity Chart similar to this, helping to expose irregularities and help manage time more efficiently*

My Hours Support

My Hours is very easy to use; just navigate to the *Support* tab on the home page, and view the My Hours tutorial video. There are also numerous links to helpful articles.

Summary

This chapter looked at two no-cost project management solutions. ProjectLibre is an open source, cross-platform program. Next, we covered Asana, a web-based project management solution that's free for up to 15 team members.

Next, you looked at MintHCM, a free, open source human resource solution for managing employee records, vacation schedules, sick leave, and other aspects of human resource management. The next item you looked at was ABC Inventory, a free (and complex but capable) program for managing inventory; this program can be a great option for a warehouse or distribution center. Finally, you explored a free, web-based solution for tracking time, an indispensable solution for solo freelancers who need to keep track of every billable hour.

In the next chapter, you'll look at several free solutions for creating websites, as well as web browsers.

CHAPTER 7

Website Creation Software and Web Browsers

This chapter introduces a couple of no-cost/low-cost tools for creating websites or blogging, as well as free web browsers for security and privacy.

Here's a look at the software programs covered in this chapter:

- **WordPress**: A tool for website and blog creation

- **Webador**: Free for individuals and hobbyists

- **AVG Secure Browser**: Browse more securely and privately

- **Firefox**: The open source browser that respects privacy

WordPress: Free, Open Source Website, Blog, and App Creation Software

Here are a few facts about WordPress at a glance:

- **Alternative to**: IM Creator

- **Website**: www.wordpress.org

- **License**: GNU General Public License

- **Current Version**: 6.0.1

- **Operating Systems**: Server running PHP (Version 7.4 or greater) and MySQL (Version 5.7) or Maria DB (Version 10.3 or greater)

Before proceeding, there is something I should first mention. This part of the chapter refers to WordPress.org (not WordPress.com).

© Phillip Whitt 2022
P. Whitt, *Pro Freeware and Open Source Solutions for Business*, https://doi.org/10.1007/978-1-4842-8841-2_7

For those that are tech savvy, the software (which is free and open source) can be downloaded from WordPress.org and installed. Then you take care of the domain name and hosting yourself. If you prefer, you may instead choose a hosting provider (such as DreamHost or Bluehost).

WordPress.com is a service that uses the WordPress software allowing you to create your own custom site. The plans range in price from personal ($4.00 per month) to e-commerce ($45.00 per month).

According to WordPress.org, it powers over 43% of the Web. At the time I wrote the first edition of this book, it was around 23%, so that's quite a leap!

Feature Highlights

Here are some noteworthy features of WordPress:

- Plug-ins: There are almost 60,000 free plug-ins to choose from to expand the range of functionality.

- Themes: You can add style to your website or blog with over 9800 free themes to choose from.

- Patterns: Adds beautiful layouts to your WordPress site.

- BuddyPress is an integral part of WordPress; it enables you to run any kind of social network on your program, with activity streams, user groups, member profiles, messaging, and much more. For more information, visit `https://buddypress.org/`.

- WP Super Cache is WordPress' extremely fast caching engine that produces static HTML files.

WordPress users may choose to install and switch between themes (Figure 7-1). Themes are what allow users to change the look and functionality of a WordPress website. They can be installed without altering the content or health of the site. WordPress websites all require at least one theme be present. WordPress themes are, in general, free themes, but the program also provides premium themes a price. Users of this program may also create and develop custom themes if they have the knowledge and skill to do so.

Figure 7-1. *There are a number of themes available in WordPress*

Other features available within WordPress consist of integrated link management; a search engine-friendly, clean perm link structure; and the ability to tag posts and articles. Automatic filters are also included, providing standardized formatting and styling of text and articles. WordPress also supports the TrackBack and Pingback standards for displaying links to other sites that have themselves linked to a post or an article. WordPress blog posts can be edited in either HTML, using the visual editor, or via a number of plug-ins that offer a wide variety of customized editing features.

Multi-User and Multi-Blogging

Before Version 3, WordPress supported one blog per installation. This was limiting, to say the least, although multiple concurrent copies were able to run from different directories, as long as they were configured to use separate database tables. WordPress Multi-User (formerly referred to as WordPress MU, or WPMU,) was almost a splitting in half of WordPress and was created to allow multiple blogs to exist within that one installation but with the ability to be administered by a centralized maintainer. WordPress MU has made it possible for those individuals with websites to host their own blogging communities and to also control and moderate all blogs from a single dashboard (Figure 7-2).

Figure 7-2. *WordPress MU makes it possible for individuals with websites to host blogging communities*

WordPress Support

A good place to start is on the *Support* tab on WordPress.org. You'll have access to the *Getting Started, Installing WordPress*, and *Basic Usage* pages. There are also forums that allow you to reach out for help. There are also plenty of tutorials on YouTube that will help.

Webador: Free for Individuals and Hobbyists

If you're looking for a basic, noncommercial website, this would be your solution. Webador offers an *Always free* plan for individuals and hobbyists. You get a webador.com address and all the essential features. There are very affordable plans for business use, ranging from $6.00 to $20.00 per month.

Here are a few facts about Webador at a glance:

- **Alternative to**: Wix

- **Website**: www.webador.com/

- **No Technical Experience Necessary**

Webador makes it easy for those with little to no technical knowledge to quickly design a website—just follow the easy steps to sign up. After you register, simply enter your name, email address, and website title to get started. Then you can design and build your website (Figure 7-3).

Figure 7-3. *After registering, you can design and build your website*

Webador Features

If you're technically challenged, Webador offers a great deal. Here are the features the website lists:

- No coding or design experience required
- Simple drag and drop approach for beginners
- Live preview of your website
- A variety of templates to choose from (50 + different templates)
- Fully customizable
- One website for desktop and mobile

- Free .webador.com address (upgrade to a *Pro* or *Business* plan to get your own domain name)

- Business email address

- Upload images and create photo albums

- Start a webshop

- Track your success with statistics

- Integrated social media

Webador Support

You can find answers to just about any question on the Webador *Help Center* page. If you can't find what you're looking for there, you can submit a *Webador Contact Form*.

There's also lots of information and tutorials on Webador's YouTube channel: www.youtube.com/c/Webador.

AVG Secure Browser: Browse More Securely and Privately

AVG Secure Browser helps make using the Internet a bit safer by adding extra privacy and security. It integrates well with AVG antivirus software (which is available in a free version).

Here are a few facts about AVG Secure Browser at a glance:

Alternative to: Google Chrome

Website: www.avg.com/en-ww/secure-browser#pc

License: Freemium

Operating System: Windows, macOS, Android, iOS

This browser is worth trying out, especially if you're still using Windows 7 and going online. Of course, Microsoft no longer supports Windows 7, so I recommend either upgrading to a newer version of Windows or trying out a Linux operating system (several Linux distributions covered in Chapter 10).

Although it's free, the license only allows you to install it on one computer (Figure 7-4). You'll need to use a paid plan to install on more than one machine.

Figure 7-4. *The free version of AVG Secure Browser's license allows installation on one computer*

When downloaded, it will automatically install on your system and you're set—you won't need to install it yourself or configure it. You can customize the look from the *Settings* menu if desired; choose from light or dark browser colors, change the font size and style, etc.

AVG Secure Browser was designed by security experts with privacy and security as the main goal. It allows you to use the Internet while protecting your computer from tracking, phishing, and other threats (Figure 7-5).

Figure 7-5. *AVG Secure Browser was designed by security experts with privacy and security in mind*

Feature Highlights

Here are the features of this browser, as listed on the provider's website:

- Private browsing mode

- Automatically blocks ads

- Seamless integration with AVG Anti-Virus and AVG Secure VPN

- Forces HTTPS encryption

- Protects you against tracking scripts

- Help manage your browser's fingerprint

- Extension guard (third-party extensions often pose a significant threat to your online security and privacy; by only installing those that you trust, we keep you better protected)

- Anti-phishing (blocks malicious websites and downloads by using our internal malware knowledge base to constantly detect threats in real time)

- Password manager (safely store, create, and autofill your login credentials for your favorite sites)

- Flash protect (automatically blocks Flash-based content from running unless you choose to allow it, to stop it from hogging computer resources)

AVG Secure Browser Support

The *AVG Signal Blog* (`www.avg.com/en/signal`) is a valuable resource for learning more about secure browsing. It explains what threats like malware, viruses, and ransomware are, what the differences are, and how to protect yourself from them.

Firefox: The Open Source Browser That Respects Privacy

Mozilla Firefox (known simply as Firefox) is a free and open source web browser developed for Windows, macOS, and Linux, with mobile versions for Android and iOS. Produced by the Mozilla Foundation and its subsidiary, the Mozilla Corporation, Firefox uses the Gecko layout engine to render web pages. Firefox implements current and anticipated web standards into its browser.

Here are a few facts about Firefox at a glance:

- **Alternative to**: Internet Explorer, Chrome

- **Website**: `www.mozilla.org/firefox`

- **Current Version**: 103.0.2 (desktop)

- **License**: MPL (Mozilla Public License) 2.0

- **Operating System**: Windows, macOS, Linux, Android, iOS

Because Firefox is free and open source, it can be installed to as many computers (or devices) as needed (Figure 7-6).

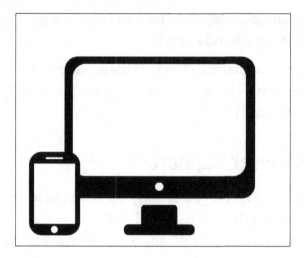

Figure 7-6. *Firefox can be installed on as many computers or devices as needed*

- Firefox offers a browser that's fast and, just as important, places a strong emphasis on protecting your privacy. Even though Google Chrome is ostensibly the number one Internet browser in the world, Firefox is an attractive alternative to those with privacy concerns.

- It states on the Mozilla website that you get all of the speed and functionality you need with privacy invasion. Since they don't have a financial stake in your information, you don't even have to provide your email address to download the installer.

Feature Highlights

Here's a look at some of the features offered in Firefox as described on the website:

- Blocks third-party tracking cookies by default

- Autoplay blocking

- Blocks social trackers

- OS availability

- In-browser screenshot tool

- Primary password

These are just a few—for a comparison to the other top web browsers, visit this page: `www.mozilla.org/en-US/firefox/browsers/compare/`.

Summary

In this chapter, we looked at a couple of options for building websites. WordPress now powers 43% of the Web and has grown into a desirable option for business over the years. Because WordPress is primarily a tool for blogging, this provides a great way for business to stay connected to their customer base. Webador offers a free plan for a personal or hobbyist website but offers affordable rates for sites better suited for business. It requires no coding knowledge, so building a site with Webador is so easy, just about anyone can do it.

We also looked at two web browsers that offer security and privacy. AVG Secure Browser was designed with privacy and security in mind and integrates well with AVG Antivirus and AVG Secure VPN. Mozilla Firefox is a popular browser that places a great deal of emphasis on privacy.

In the next chapter, we'll look at some free content management solutions.

CHAPTER 8

Content Management Solutions

This chapter takes a look at the following alternatives to expensive CMS programs such as Microsoft SharePoint:

- **Drupal**: An open source, community-based alternative
- **ConcreteCMS**: An open source content management system
- **GetSimple CMS**: A simple, open source content management system

Drupal: An Open Source, Community-Based Alternative

Drupal is one of the world's leading web content management applications. It allows users to easily organize, manage, and publish their content with a seemingly endless variety of customization. Drupal is open source software that is developed and maintained by a group of over one million users and developers. Because it is distributed under the terms of the GNU General Public license, it's free for anyone to download and share with others. This open development model means that individuals are continuously working to make sure Drupal is a cutting-edge platform that can support the latest technologies offered on the World Wide Web. The Drupal project's principles encourage standards, modularity, ease of use, and collaboration.

Here are a few facts about Drupal at a glance:

- **Alternative to**: Microsoft SharePoint
- **Website**: `www.drupal.org`
- **License**: GPL Version 2 or Later

© Phillip Whitt 2022
P. Whitt, *Pro Freeware and Open Source Solutions for Business*, https://doi.org/10.1007/978-1-4842-8841-2_8

- **Current Version**: 9.4

- **Operating System**: Cross-platform

- **Potential Savings**: $6.00 per user per month (not counting hosting costs)

Drupal is used as a backend framework for many of the many websites used worldwide (according to BuiltWith, there are around 1,764,551 websites using Drupal: `https://trends.builtwith.com/cms/Drupal`). This includes sites ranging from personal blogs to corporate, political, and government sites. It is also recognized for business collaboration and knowledge management.

Drupal Core contains basic features commonly found in most content management systems. These features include user account registration and maintenance, managing menus, taxonomy, customized page layouts, RSS feeds, and system administration.

There are currently over 49,000 free community-contributed add-ons, known as contributed modules. These are available to alter and/or extend Drupal's capabilities and to add new features or customize the program's behavior and appearance.

The Drupal community has in excess of one million members; according to the website, this includes developers, designers, trainers, strategists, coordinators, editors, and sponsors working together.

Feature Highlights

The following are some of the features offered by Drupal:

- **Mobile friendly**: Built-in themes and administration pages are quite easy to use on mobile devices. The new admin toolbar is mobile from the start. Tables shrink properly. The new administration properties feature a back-to-site button that leads back to the last front-end page.

- **Multilingual capabilities**: When you need to establish a web presence for a global audience, Drupal 8 can speak your language, whatever it may be. This application can translate anything in the system with the built-in user interfaces. Another great facet of the program is that you can get software translation updates automatically from the Drupal community.

- **Configuration management**: CM keeps accurate records of all important details as content is configured and/or revised. This program comes with a file system based on the CM system, which makes it simple to transport configuration changes, such as new content types, fields, or views, from development to production.

- **Accessibility**: For standard accessibility technologies, including WAIARIA, Drupal 8 has added extensive support, and developers have been working to provide more semantic HTML5.

Bug Smash Initiative

The Bug Smash Initiative is a community-driven effort to fix known bugs in Drupal Core (Figure 8-1). There's no formal membership, and anyone can join. To date, over 2700 bugs have been "smashed." For more information about the Bug Smash Initiative, visit this page: `www.drupal.org/community-initiatives/bug-smash-initiative`.

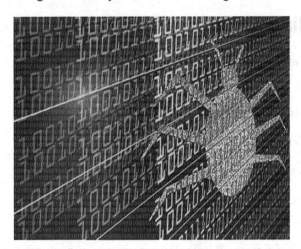

Figure 8-1. *The Bug Smash Initiative is a community-driven effort to fix known bugs in Drupal Core*

Drupal Support

Because Drupal is so actively supported, there is lots of help available. The *Support* page (`www.drupal.org/support`) points the way to discussion forums, books, community documentation, and more. There are also plenty of Drupal tutorial videos on YouTube.

ConcreteCMS: An Open Source Content Management System

The free and open source ConcreteCMS is a content management system for publishing content on the Web and on an intranet. For those seeking a viable alternative to Microsoft SharePoint, this is well worth investigating.

- **Alternative to**: Microsoft SharePoint

- **Website**: www.concretecms.com/

- **License**: MIT

- **Current Version:** 9.1.1

- **Potential savings**: $5.00 per user per month (not counting hosting costs)

Feature Highlights

Here is a quick look at some of the features offered by ConcreteCMS as shown on the website:

- Makes editing your website should be as easy as writing a document.

- You can train up new content editors in just minutes.

- Your work will be better when your tools are a joy to use.

- You have complete control over who can do what to any part of any page with ConcreteCMS.

- Approval workflows will help you empower your editors to do more on their own safely.

- You can easily allow many people to collaborate on your website.

- You get a fully ISO:27001 solution out of the box.

- SOC 2 compliance standard with all our hosting.

- Used by the US Army. Choose to host your site with us to meet any unique compliance and security needs your organization may have.

ConcreteCMS Essentials

One of the essential features in ContreteCMS is a WYSIWYG editor, allowing you to customize your site exactly the way you want it to look with no coding needed (Figure 8-2).

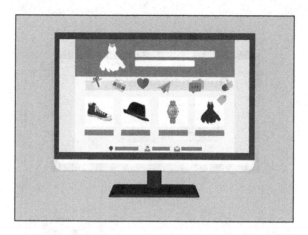

Figure 8-2. *ConcreteCMS offers a WYSIWYG editor, allowing to customize your site exactly as you want it*

There are a wide variety of add-ons available allowing you to extend your site and expand its functionality. This allows a great deal of flexibility in your site.

ConcreteCMS also offers several marketing tools. It allows you to create forms and surveys for data collection. It offers the ability to create forms that integrate with popular CRM programs. With integrated reporting, all of your data is in one interface, allowing you to make marketing decisions with greater ease.

With ConcreteCMS, you can add customizable blogs to your website. Some of the features offered are Rss syndication, category support, topics, multiple authors, likes, and post display options.

The commenting system supports threaded comments and has the ability to moderate comments and authenticate the commenter, use avatars, detect spam, enable or disable anonymous commenting, and sort through comments.

While ConcreteCMS is free and open source, it requires paying a service to host your site. You can opt to use the ConcreteCMS Hosting Service. If you're on a budget, you can use a cheaper service that ConcreteCMS partners with (such as HostDash or A2 Hosting).

ConcreteCMS Support

There is a great deal of support for ConcreteCMS. One source of help is the User Guide (Figure 8-3) on the *Support* page: `https://documentation.concretecms.org/`.

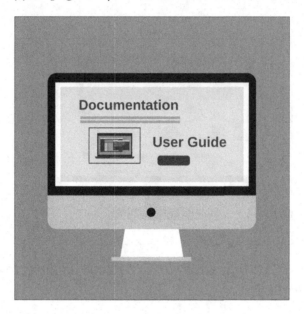

Figure 8-3. *The User Guide can be accessed from the Support page*

Also on the Support page are links to several video tutorials. ConcreteCMS also maintains a YouTube channel with several video tutorials.

GetSimple CMS: A Simple, Open Source Content Management System

If Drupal or ConcreteCMS is more than you need, then GetSimple CMS might be more your speed. GetSimple CMS (not to be confused with GetSimple.net, a web hosting service) is a free and open source website content management system. GetSimple CMS focuses more on simplicity and ease of use while excluding features that you don't need.

Here are a few facts about GetSimple CMS at a glance:

- **Website**: `http://get-simple.info`

- **License**: GPL 3, Open Source, Get-Simple.info

- **Operating System**: Cross-platform

GetSimple CMS is intended to be simple, fast, and easy to use. Based on PHP and released under the General Public license (GNU), GetSimple saves all data to structured XML files instead of using a database to store information. By doing this, it makes the application belong to the group of flat file web applications, which can be run without a database. Important to note, the system's memory footprint is low, which makes it suitable to be installed within a shared hosting situation. It provides online documentation in a wiki form, and an active community can be located on the GetSimple website.

Feature Highlights

Here are some of the features offered by GetSimple CMS, as stated on the website:

- **XML Based:** We don't use mySQL to store our information but instead depend on the simplicity of XML. By utilizing XML, we are able to stay away from introducing an extra layer of slowness and complexity associated with connecting to a mySQL database. Because GetSimple was built specifically for the small-site market, we feel this is the absolutely best option for data storage.

- **You can "Undo" Almost Everything:** This feature was based off an eye-opening AListApart article explaining how warning messages never work as planned. Because of this, we've included "undo" into almost every action you can take on the site, giving you peace of mind for when you make those inevitable stupid mistakes.

- **Easy to Learn UI:** The top priority when designing our user interface was to make it the best in its class. We had the luxury of trying and testing all the competing management systems before designing ours, so we took the best out of each one and then refined it.

- **Simple Installation:** The total time in setting up a website took a total of 5 minutes, from starting the FTP to finishing the setup procedure.

- **Simple Theme Customization:** We have how to documents that show you how to create a custom theme. Our goal was not to bloat our software with hundreds of little-used theme functions but to offer more than enough to allow for a fully customized theme.

- **Designed For the Small-Site Market:** This is one of the reasons GetSimple uses XML rather than a robust database such as mySQL. For most small businesses, their only real need is to be able to easily update their site without the need of a ton of extraneous rarely used features. GetSimple's goal is to manage small websites efficiently and effectively.

The original concept was simply to provide a way to maintain a website without knowledge of HTML via a program that presented a clear, user-friendly interface. In order to create a new GetSimple website, you must know how to use FTP and have a basic knowledge of HTML.

Once you upload the system files to a web server, the setup is complete. The final configuration is made easy by using the system's web-based install wizard; some hosting providers offer preconfigured GetSimple installations.

An XML-based, stand-alone program that doesn't use MySQL to store information, GetSimple is a fully independent and light content management system. The interface has been loaded with features that every website needs, but with nothing it doesn't. It is considered by most to be truly the simplest way to manage a small business website. Since it doesn't need a MySQL database, it was built specifically for the small site market.

To prevent problems, GetSimple has included "undo" into almost every action you can take, keeping you free from headaches when those inevitable mistakes are made. Since you can "undo" pretty much anything you do, this feature is based on eye-opening ideas such as explaining how warning messages never work as planned.

Because it was specifically designed for the small site market, GetSimple utilizes XML rather than a larger, perhaps overwhelming, database such as MySQL. The majority of small businesses only need to be able to easily update the site; they don't require many extraneous and rarely used features. GetSimple's ultimate goal is to assist in managing small websites efficiently and effectively.

GetSimple CMS Support

The best place to start is the Documentation and User Guide Wiki. There you will find information about what GetSimple CMS is for, what others are saying about it, and getting started.

There is an active community on the Support Forum where help can be sought out if needed. Additionally, there are also several helpful video tutorials on YouTube that will get you up and running in short order.

Summary

In this chapter, you looked at three free options for content management systems. For those seeking alternatives to paid systems, Drupal, ConcreteCMS, and GetSimple CMS are great options.

In the next chapter, you'll take a look at several options for network security, password security, and free antivirus programs.

CHAPTER 9

Network and Security Utilities

Security is always a high priority in business. If you're on budget, but you require solutions for areas such as network security, password security, antivirus, and mobile device privacy, there are some no-cost options. Here's a look at the software programs covered in this chapter.

Network Security Auditing

- **Nmap:** A free and open source utility for network discovery and security auditing

Password Management

- **KeePass:** A free and open source password manager that can be helpful for keeping your passwords secure if you have an online presence

Packet Analyzer

- **tcpdump:** A powerful command-line packet analyzer

Antivirus Protection

- **Avira:** Powerful, free antivirus protection for PC and Mac

- **Clam AV:** An open source cross-platform antivirus solution

201

© Phillip Whitt 2022
P. Whitt, *Pro Freeware and Open Source Solutions for Business*, https://doi.org/10.1007/978-1-4842-8841-2_9

Android and iPhone Privacy

- **Open Whisper Systems:** Open source security for mobile devices that helps keep your texts and conversations private and secure

Nmap: A Free and Open Source Utility for Network Discovery/Security Auditing

The primary purpose of the Nmap application is security auditing by detecting and locating hosts and services on any given computer network (Figure 9-1). In order to do this, Nmap sends packets that are specifically tailored to the target host, at which point the responses are analyzed. Host discovery and service, and operating system detection, are among the many features Nmap offers for probing computer networks. During a scan, Nmap acclimates to various network conditions, such as latency and congestion. While a professional developer originally wrote this software, Nmap is now further developed and refined by the user community.

Figure 9-1. Nmap conducts security audits by detecting and locating hosts and services on computer networks

Nmap is commonly used to audit the security of a device or firewall by identifying the potential network connections. Determining open ports on a target host is another regular use, as are network inventory, network mapping, maintenance, and asset management. While identifying new servers and generating traffic, the security is regularly being audited by finding and exploiting vulnerabilities in a network.

Some facts about Nmap at a glance:

- **Website:** `https://nmap.org`

- **License:** GPL Version 2

- **Current Version:** 7.92

- **Operating System:** Cross-platform

Users will find many benefits to using Nmap. For example, it has a simple installation and front end. With minimal effort, it will give a strong result, making it one of the easiest software products available. Nmap will map the network and ports with the number one port scanning tool.

Feature Highlights

Here are the features offered by Nmap as listed on their website:

- **Flexible**: Supports dozens of advanced techniques for mapping out networks filled with IP filters, firewalls, routers, and other obstacles. This includes many port scanning mechanisms (both TCP and UDP), OS detection, version detection, ping sweeps, and more. See the documentation page.

- **Powerful**: Nmap has been used to scan huge networks of literally hundreds of thousands of machines.

- **Portable**: Most operating systems are supported, including Linux, Microsoft Windows, FreeBSD, OpenBSD, Solaris, IRIX, macOS X, HP-UX, NetBSD, Sun OS, Amiga, and more.

- **Easy**: While Nmap offers a rich set of advanced features for power users, you can start out as simply as "nmap -v -A *targethost*". Both traditional command-line and graphical (GUI) versions are available to suit your preference. Binaries are available for those who do not wish to compile Nmap from source.

- **Free**: The primary goals of the Nmap project are to help make the Internet a little more secure and to provide administrators/auditors/ hackers with an advanced tool for exploring their networks. Nmap is available for free download and also comes with full source code that you may modify and redistribute under the terms of the license.

- **Well Documented**: Significant effort has been put into comprehensive and up-to-date man pages, whitepapers, tutorials, and even a whole book! Find them in multiple languages here.

- **Supported**: While Nmap comes with no warranty, it is well supported by a vibrant community of developers and users. Most of this interaction occurs on the Nmap mailing lists. Most bug reports and questions should be sent to the nmap-dev list, but only after you read the guidelines. We recommend that all users subscribe to the low-traffic nmap-hackers announcement list. You can also find Nmap on Facebook and Twitter. For real-time chat, join the #nmap channel on Freenode or EFNet.

- **Acclaimed**: Nmap has won numerous awards, including "Information Security Product of the Year" by *Linux Journal*, InfoWorld, and Codetalker Digest. It has been featured in hundreds of magazine articles, several movies, dozens of books, and one comic book series. Visit the press page for further details.

- **Popular**: Thousands of people download Nmap every day, and it is included with many operating systems (Redhat Linux, Debian Linux, Gentoo, FreeBSD, OpenBSD, etc.). It is among the top 10 (out of 30,000) programs at the Freshmeat.Net repository. This is important because it lends Nmap its vibrant development and user support communities.

Nmap was created to quickly scan large networks. It is because of this that it is regularly used for network inventory security audits. While doing this, the user is able to see what types of services a host is using. It is quite remarkable that when one scans a large network, the hosts appear; and for each one, data is provided regarding which OS is running, the service and version of that OS, which firewall is used, etc. This information is meaningful because some older versions may have known security issues that could damage the entire machine. Armed with this knowledge, you can update to the latest version, decreasing the potential for harm.

Nmap displays detected ports in a table. For each port that is detected, a list of the port's number, protocol, state, and version is displayed. The state can be listed as open, closed, filtered, or unfiltered. The difference between open and closed ports is that open ports listen for packets or connections on that port, while there is no such service on closed ports. On filtered ports, there is a firewall blocking Nmap, preventing it from detecting if it is open or closed. When the port is responsive to Nmap's probes (but whether open or closed is undetermined), Nmap will classify that port as unfiltered. While this does occasionally happen, it is very rare; the status of ports usually falls under the categories of open, closed, or filtered.

Nmap offers additional information on targets. This could consist of reverse DNS names, device types, operating system guesses, and MAC addresses. Finding a MAC address and reverse DNS appear to be the most highly utilized features by consumers. Nmap's attempts to guess the OS can be a bit hit-and-miss, but that occurs even with expensive programs.

For those new to Nmap, the front end is convenient. You can easily use it to pass different preconfigured parameters to Nmap without remembering any commands, and it offers a comprehensive set of options. A convenient feature is that the program highlights some of the info in different colors so you can read it easier.

There are many benefits to using Nmap. To begin, it is powerful enough to satisfy most individual's needs but it offers a simple installation process. It is also one of the smallest software packages of its kind (0.6 MB) and can be easily deployed in mini-distributions. Nmap is considered one of the best software applications for security auditing, and it can definitely be a good starting point for people who want to explore security options.

Nmap Support

Becoming familiar with the *Reference Guide* is always recommended. There are a good number of tutorial videos on YouTube that should prove useful.

KeePass: A Free and Open Source Password Manager

KeePass is a vital security management tool. Professionals suggest that one of the most important things to do is to protect one's online security. Assigning a unique, lengthy, randomized password for every single site or account you use, and keeping track of the all those passwords, would pose a challenge for even the most organized person. This is where KeePass comes in handy.

KeePass is a free and open source password manager that is compatible with the following: Windows, Linux, Android, macOS X, and with unofficial ports for iOS.

Here are a few facts about KeePass at a glance:

- **Alternative to:** Steganos Password Manager 16

- **Website:** www.keepass.info

- **License:** GNU GPL Version 2+

- **Current Version:** 2.51

- **Operating Systems:** Windows, macOS, Linux

- **Potential Savings:** $24.99 for up to five PCs

KeePass is free and open source software (and is OSI certified). It can be installed on as many computers as needed (Figure 9-2).

Figure 9-2. *KeePass can be installed on as many computers as needed*

KeePass is a very handy application. Instead of writing passwords down here and there (and worrying about where they are when you can't find them), KeePass assists you by storing all of your passwords securely in the program's database. You need to remember only one "master" password to access your stored passwords (Figure 9-3).

Figure 9-3. *KeePass stores all of the passwords you create, so you only need to remember one master password*

Feature Highlights

Here are the main features of KeePass:

- **Password management:** Passwords stored in this application's database can be further divided into manageable groups. Each group can have its own separate identifying icon.

- **Extensible:** Offers a number of different configuration options.

- **Tracks passwords:** KeePass tracks the creation time, modification time, last access time, and expiration time of each password stored, allowing you to attach and store a password on files and text notes.

- **Import and export:** The password list is exportable to various formats, such as TXT, HTML, XML, and CSV.

- **Multiuser support:** This application supports simultaneous access and changes to a shared password file by utilizing multiple computers, often using a shared network drive.

- **Autotype, global hotkeys, drag-and-drop:** KeePass provides support for these features. KeePass can minimize itself and type the information of the currently selected entry into such things as dialogs, web forms, etc.

- **Browser support:** The available autotype functionality works very well with all browsers. There is a KeeForm extension that allows users to open websites with Internet Explorer and Mozilla Firefox. For Firefox, there is an additional extension called KeeFox, which will automatically connect to KeePass when a user needs access to a password.

- **Built-in password generator:** This generates random passwords, and random seating is available for user input.

- **Plug-ins:** KeePass possesses a plug-in architecture, and there are a variety of plug-ins available on the KeePass homepage. One thing to bear in mind is that plug-ins may compromise the security of KeePass because they are written by independent authors, and these authors have full access to the database while developing their plug-ins.

Unlike other competitors, KeePass doesn't automatically put your password database in the cloud, although another option is to put your password into Dropbox manually.

KeePass presents its own random password generator to ensure the user doesn't have to take on the arduous task of coming up with, and then remembering, countless lengthy, complex passwords on their own. Additionally, KeePass includes a quick-search box where one can type even a fragment of a website's name to quickly find it on the list. The list itself is created to contain thousands of records, which can be subdivided into folders and subfolders, keeping things organized.

KeePass isn't just limited to usernames and passwords; every entry has multiple alternate fields, one of which is a free-form Notes field which allows the safe storing of text of any kind.

One technique hackers use to circumvent password protection is to use a keylogger. A keylogger is a background application that secretly logs every keystroke that is typed, and that information is transmitted to the hacker. If a keylogger is installed on a user's system, an attacker could conceivably learn everything that was typed throughout the day, including all usernames and passwords.

Another protection feature that KeePass offers is its *AutoType* feature. This feature prevents the user from having to type individual website passwords by pasting them into the browser window and applying a combination of virtual keystrokes and clipboard obfuscation, making it all the more difficult for a keylogger to figure out what the password actually is. While AutoType can be temperamental, when it does work, it's extremely useful.

KeePass also lets the user enter their master database password in a prompt that is protected by UAC. This protects it from any software keylogger that isn't running with Administrator rights on the machine.

KeePass is recommended to anyone with an online presence (no matter how small) because, when a major website has its security breached, users of KeePass are unaffected, knowing their personal information remains safe and secure.

In summation, KeePass is a quality, easy-to-use, password protection system. There seem to be few bugs with the program, but there are many great security benefits. Whether a business or an individual, extra password protection is very important, especially in these times of rampant hacking. KeePass can offer peace of mind regarding your computer's safety.

KeePass Support

KeePass is a relatively easy program to come to grips with, but if you get stuck, the *Help Center* can be found at `http://keepass.info/help`. The FAQ page is another source of assistance, as are the numerous YouTube tutorials.

tcpdump: A Powerful Command-Line Packet Analyzer

tcpdump was designed for users that need to analyze network traffic by capturing packets from a certain adapter. It is a network sniffer tool, and it can capture all the data packets that are transmitted or received through a network adapter. The program is executable in command-line mode, and it allows the user to perform multiple actions by using arguments.

Information regarding captured packets may be viewed in real time using the command prompt window or recorded to a log file to assist in analyzing the packets at a later date.

Here are a few facts about tcpdump at a glance:

- **Website:** www.tcpdump.org/

- **License:** BSD License

- **Current Version:**4.99.1 / libpcap 1.10.1

- **Operating System(s):** Linux, Solaris, FreeBSD, NetBSD, Open BSD, OS X, Android, AIX, and others

tcpdump works on most UNIX-like operating systems (see above). When used in those systems, tcpdump uses the libpcap library to capture packets. The software provider's website indicates that the port utilized by tcpdump for Windows is called WinDump, which uses WinPcap, the Windows port of libpcap.

Feature Highlights

Here are a few of the features found in this program:

- **Powerful command-line packet analyzer:** tcpdump works with libpcap, a portable C/C++ library, for network traffic capture.

- **Can run remotely:** Through an SSH or Telnet.

- **Writes packets to standard output/file:** tcpdump prints the contents of network packets, and it can also read packets from a network interface card or even from a previously created saved packet file.

- **Monitor communications:** It is possible to use this program for the specific purpose of intercepting and displaying the communications of another user or computer.

- **Optional BPF-based filter:** The user may add this filter to limit the number of packets seen by tcpdump. This does render the output more usable on networks with a high volume of traffic.

The information on the software provider's website indicates that tcpdump works on most UNIX-like operating systems. When used in those systems, tcpdump uses the libpcap library to capture packets. The port utilized by tcpdump for Windows is called WinDump, which uses WinPcap, the Windows port of libpcap.

tcpdump Support

The documentation for tcpdump (`www.tcpdump.org/faq.html`) is a good starting point, and the FAQ is also a source of help (`www.tcpdump.org/faq.html`). There are quite a few video introductions and tutorials on YouTube as well.

Avira: Powerful, Free Antivirus Protection for Personal PCs and Macs

Avira Operations GmbH & Co. KG is a German multinational-owned antivirus software company. It provides IT security for computers, smartphones, servers, and networks, which can be delivered as both software and cloud-based services.

A few facts about Avira at a glance:

- **Alternative to:** McAfee AntiVirus Plus

- **Website:** `www.avira.com`

- **License:** Proprietary Freeware

- **Current Version:** 1.1.35.25717

- **Operating System(s):** Windows, macOS

- **Potential Savings:** $34.99 (McAfee annual subscription)

If you have a personal computer you use in a non-production environment, then the free version of Avira might be just what you need. The free version of Avira can be installed on one PC or one Mac (Figure 9-4).

Figure 9-4. *The free version of Avira can be installed on one PC or one Mac in a non-production environment*

Feature Highlights

Here are a few of the features found in this program as described on their website:

- Blocks spyware, ransomware, and phishing attacks.

- Secures and anonymizes your web browsing.

- Boosts your computer's performance and cleans junk files.

It's quite clear through customer and critic ratings, and actual downloads, that Avira is a popular product. The company has been around for enough years to have refined their business model, and it provides a comprehensive, useful tool for individuals for free. They have found their niche field, and by not continuously delving into other areas of IT and software, they've stayed focused and on point on antivirus applications in other related programs.

Avira Support

Avira is an easy program to install and run. However, Avira does not offer support on the free version of their antivirus program. There are a number of YouTube videos that you should find helpful.

ClamAV: An Open Source Cross-Platform (Including Linux) Antivirus Program

ClamAV is a cross-platform, free, open source antivirus software toolkit used by millions of people. It is capable of detecting a wide variety of malicious software, including viruses.

Here are a few facts about ClamAV at a glance:

- **Website:** www.clamav.net

- **License:** GPL

- **Current Version:** 0.105.1

- **Operating System(s):** Windows, macOS, Linux, BSD, Solaris

A primary purpose of ClamAV is on mail servers, where it acts as a server-side email virus scanner (Figure 9-5). ClamAV was created for Unix, but third-party versions are available for AIX, HP-UX, Linux, BSD, OS X, OpenVMS, Solaris, and OSF (True 64). Starting with version 0.97.5, ClamAV is also available for Microsoft Windows. Not only is the initial program free, but future updates will be available at no cost.

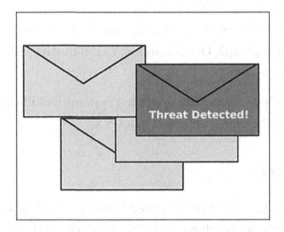

Figure 9-5.   *ClamAV serves well as a server-side email scanner*

The ClamAV engine can be dependably used to identify several kinds of files. Specifically, some phishing emails can be exposed using antivirus techniques. For Linux systems, it provides real-time protection. According to the information on the website, it detects millions of viruses and other types of threats; this includes Microsoft Office macro viruses.

Feature Highlights

Here are some of the feature highlights as shown on the ClamAV website:

- ClamAV is designed to scan files quickly.

- Real-time protection (Linux only). The ClamOnAcc client for the ClamD scanning daemon provides on-access scanning on modern versions of Linux. This includes an optional capability to block file access until a file has been scanned (on-access prevention).

- ClamAV detects millions of viruses, worms, trojans, and other malware, including Microsoft Office macro viruses, mobile malware, and other threats.

- ClamAV's bytecode signature runtime, powered by either LLVM or our custom bytecode interpreter, allows the ClamAV signature writers to create and distribute very complex detection routines and remotely enhance the scanner's functionality.

- Signed signature databases ensure that ClamAV will only execute trusted signature definitions.

- :Built-in support for various archive formats, including ZIP, RAR, DMG, Tar, Gzip, Bzip2, OLE2, Cabinet, CHM, BinHex, SIS, and many others.

- Can be installed on all major operating systems including Linux, Windows, BSD, Solaris, and even macOS X.

ClamAV Support

The documentation for ClamAV can be viewed here: `https://docs.clamav.net/`. There are numerous YouTube tutorials that cover ClamAV, particularly for Linux distributions.

Signal: Open Source Security for Mobile Devices

Signal is a nonprofit group of software developers whose primary goal is to provide security and privacy for mobile devices.

Here are a few facts about Signal at a glance:

- **Website:** https://signal.org/en/#signal

- **License:** GPL

- **Operating System(s):** Android, iPhone, iPad, Windows, macOS, and Linux

According to the website, Signal is used by several prominent people, including whistleblower and privacy advocate Edward Snowden and Twitter CEO Jack Dorsey. Signal is open source and can be used for phones, iPads, and desktop computers (Figure 9-6).

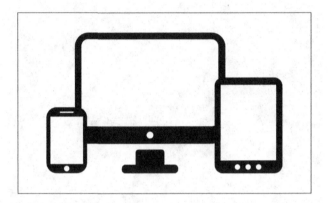

Figure 9-6. *Signal can provide security for multiple devices*

Feature Highlights

Here are the highlights (slightly abridged) as shown on Signal's website:

- State-of-the-art end-to-end encryption (powered by the open source Signal Protocol) keeps your conversations secure. We can't read your messages or listen to your calls, and no one else can either.

- Share text, voice messages, photos, videos, GIFs, and files for free. Signal uses your phone's data connection so you can avoid SMS and MMS fees.

- Make crystal-clear voice and video calls to people who live across town, or across the ocean, with no long-distance charges.

- Add a new layer of expression to your conversations with encrypted stickers. You can also create and share your own sticker packs.

- Group chats make it easy to stay connected to your family, friends, and coworkers.

- There are no ads, no affiliate marketers, and no creepy tracking in Signal.

Signal is a nonprofit organization dedicated to privacy and is supported by grants and donations. It is not connected to any of the major technology companies and is free for everyone (Figure 9-7).

Figure 9-7. *Signal is supported by grants and donations and is freely available to anyone*

There is a technical information page with specifications and software libraries for developers. It provides links to the documents for XEdDSA and VXEdDSA, X3DH, Double Ratchet, and Sesame. The page can be viewed here: `https://signal.org/docs/`.

Signal Support

On the *Support* page, you can type in a question or search term, and you'll be directed to the forum where topics related to yours are displayed. You'll also have access to numerous articles covering various aspects such as general questions, security, etc. Although there don't seem to be many video tutorials on YouTube, there are one or two that provide some general information.

Summary

In this chapter, you looked a several solutions for various security measures. Nmap provides network auditing and detection. KeePass is an excellent program that manages important passwords and keeps them secure; you only need to keep up with a master password, and not worry about remembering the rest.

Analyzing packets with tcpdump allows the user to display the packets being transmitted or received on a network. Avira (although licensed only for personal use) is an excellent, free antivirus program ideal for computers that don't frequent the Internet very much. ClamAV is an open source antivirus program that can be installed on numerous operating systems. Signal provides security for Android mobile phones and Apple iPhones to help keep texts and conversations secure and private.

In the next chapter, you'll look at several Linux distributions, which, for many users throughout the world, are viable alternatives to the Windows and Mac computer operating systems.

CHAPTER 10

Linux: The Free Alternative to Windows and macOS

Microsoft Windows and Macintosh need no introduction. Certainly, most readers of this book are using Windows and the others are no doubt using a Mac. You may be wondering why anyone would consider using a different operating system. While Linux isn't for everyone, it offers some advantages that are well worth considering, such as security and free software.

This chapter introduces the reader to Linux: what it is, how it is used, and a brief history about how it came into existence. We'll then look at the advantages Linux offers over its well-known proprietary counterparts.

This chapter provides an in-depth look at Ubuntu, ostensibly the most popular Linux distribution in the world. We'll also take a brief look at two other Linux distributions: Zorin OS and Linux Mint.

What Is Linux?

The odds are good that you've heard of Linux and know that it's related to computers. First, it should be pointed out that Linux actually refers to the *kernel*, or "core" code around which Linux distributions are built.

Essentially, Linux is a Unix-like computer operating system that falls under the model of free and open source software development and distribution, just like the open source software discussed in this book. There are many variations of Linux known

© Phillip Whitt 2022
P. Whitt, *Pro Freeware and Open Source Solutions for Business*, https://doi.org/10.1007/978-1-4842-8841-2_10

as distributions, or *distros* as they're called in the parlance of those active in the Linux communities. With a few exceptions, Linux distributions are available at no cost (but donations are gladly accepted).

This is a short *Complete Beginner's Guide to Linux* that can be read here: `www.linux.com/training-tutorials/complete-beginners-guide-linux/`.

Linux plays a major role behind the scenes of a number of products you probably know. The ubiquitous Android operating system of millions of mobile devices (Figure 10-1) is based on the Linux kernel.

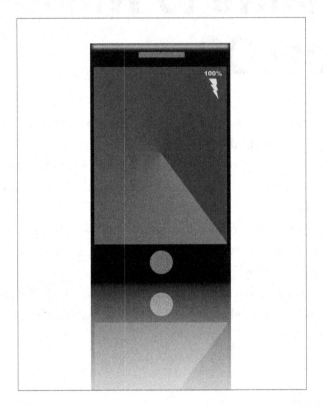

Figure 10-1. *Android mobile devices are among the numerous Linux-based products*

Linux is the force behind millions of laptop and desktop computers all over the world. One of the most popular distributions (if not *the* most popular) is Ubuntu (Figure 10-2). There are many other popular Linux distributions as well: Debian (the distribution upon which Ubuntu is derived), Linux Mint, Zorin, Fedora, and others.

Figure 10-2. *Ubuntu is a highly popular Linux distribution used on millions of computers*

Note   According to an article in It's FOSS (Munif Tanjim, December 16, 2016), the Italian city of Vicenza (at the time) was replacing Windows with Linux Zorin—the article can be read here: `https://itsfoss.com/vicenza-windows-zorin/`.

In addition to mobile devices, electronic products, laptops, and desktop computers, Linux also runs many of the servers in use (Figure 10-3). IBM provides full Linux support for all of its server platforms. Ubuntu Server is significant; according to Ubuntu's website, "Ubuntu Server is the world's leading cloud guest OS, running the majority of workloads in public clouds today, thanks to its security, versatility, and regular updates."

Figure 10-3. *Many servers in use are powered by Linux*

The majority of Linux distributions use a GUI (graphical user interface). There are several desktop environments that vary from one Linux distribution to another. The Zorin OS (which is covered in greater detail later in this chapter) is a Linux distribution that can be configured to resemble the look of Windows (Figure 10-4) to ease newcomers into Linux.

Figure 10-4.   *The Zorin OS can be configured to resemble the look of Windows. (Used with permission © The Zorin OS Team 2022)*

Linux systems typically employ a command-line feature called the *terminal* (Figure 10-5). It resembles the DOS interface that predates Microsoft Windows. The terminal provides the user access to the system underneath the graphical interface. Although many Linux users go through their computing lives without ever (or rarely) using this command-line interface, there are occasions when using it is necessary (such as the installation of certain software programs). It's a good idea for new Linux users to become familiar with the terminal feature.

Figure 10-5. *The terminal command-line feature*

Ubuntu's website provides useful details about using the terminal (Figure 10-6). To learn more, go to `https://help.ubuntu.com/community/UsingTheTerminal`.

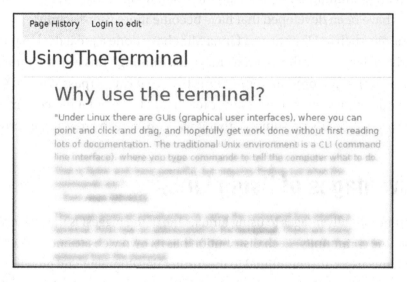

Figure 10-6. *The Ubuntu website provides useful details about using the terminal*

A Brief History of Linux

The history of Linux is actually a fairly long story, so I will provide a very short synopsis. The origin of Linux goes back to 1991 when a Finnish student at the University of Helsinki named Linus Torvalds was working on a personal project. He was developing a free operating system kernel that anyone could build upon. Around the same time, the GNU project started by Richard Stallman in 1983 was developing a free Unix-like operating system. They were near completion but were lacking a kernel for the operating system. Eventually, the two projects were integrated and a complete operating system was born. If you're interested in reading a more detailed account, go to the GNU Operating System website at www.gnu.org and click the tab titled *A Historical Overview of GNU.*

Note   According to the GNU Operating System website (and despite the fact that the term Linux is so widely used), the proper designation for the operating system is GNU/Linux. Also, the terms *distribution* and *operating system* are used synonymously in the Linux world.

In the early days of Linux, it required operators who were knowledgeable in computer programming to use it. Because it fell under the terms of the GNU License, anyone with programming skills could alter it to suit their needs. Over the years, many distributions have been developed that have become more user-friendly.

Distributions such as Ubuntu and Linux Mint have done a great deal to increase the popularity of Linux over the past several years. Although this is debatable (at least, for the time being), some proponents of Linux believe it will surpass Windows as a mainstream operating system. It may never reach that level, but it has certainly made some great strides, and it's presumable that it will continue to grow and improve.

The Advantages of Using Linux

There are numerous advantages to using Linux. One of the biggest is the availability of support from the community. Each distribution has its own website and user community forum, and Linux users are committed to the further development and growth of their preferred distribution. Some people (myself included) use more than one Linux distribution.

Here are several other advantages that using a Linux operating system offers:

- **With a few exceptions, Linux distributions are free.** Most Linux distributions are free to install; use it on one or multiple computers without paying licensing fees.

- **Try it out without installing.** Most Linux distributions can be tried out on your computer (without installing anything or making changes) by using a live CD, DVD, or USB stick. When using a live disc, the response time is much slower, but it does provide a general experience of trying it out. If you decide to, you can install Linux from the live disc or USB stick.

- **Linux is highly secure and stable.** Generally speaking, Linux systems aren't besieged with the number of viruses, Trojan horses, and malware that plague Windows. While Linux isn't always immune to these problems (and antivirus protection is always warranted), because most attacks target Windows systems, there are far fewer malicious programs that wreak havoc with Linux systems. Another perk is that Linux-based operating systems tend to be very stable and reliable.

- **There are many software titles available to suit most purposes.** Linux distributions typically come bundled with useful software, such as GIMP, LibreOffice, and other titles. Software is easy to acquire by using the distribution's *software repositories*. Some software titles are available for a small fee, and many others are free.

- **Strong community support.** Each Linux distribution has a community of users that are willing to help newcomers. There are also plenty of overview and instructional videos on YouTube covering just about every Linux distribution.

- **Install Linux alongside your current operating system.** Many people decide that they like Linux but can't bring themselves to give up Windows. The good news is, you don't have to. Linux systems can typically be installed alongside your Windows (or Mac) operating system. With a dual boot system, you'll be presented with a choice of which operating system to launch.

- **Older computers can be revitalized with Linux.** There are several lightweight Linux distributions (such as Puppy Linux or Lubuntu) that run well on older computers that are too underpowered for most modern operating systems (but are otherwise perfectly good machines). This is a great way to recycle older computers and relegate them to light duty, such as email, surfing the Web, and word processing (Figure 10-7).

Figure 10-7. *Older, lower spec computers can be revitalized by using one of the lightweight Linux distributions and relegating them to light duty, such as email, web browsing, and word processing*

Another distinct advantage of Linux is that if you aren't satisfied with a particular distribution, you can always try another one; it doesn't cost anything except a little investment in time and perhaps a blank DVD. Each distribution has its strengths and weaknesses, so it's important to use the one that serves you in the best way possible. A helpful website to compare Linux distributions is DisrtoWatch.com (`http://distrowatch.com`). Simply select the distribution you're interested in, and it provides a summary, relevant websites, popularity, etc.

Another resource to help the newcomer become better acquainted with Linux in general is the *New User Guides* page of the Linux.com website (`www.linux.com/learn/new-user-guides`).

The next section of this chapter looks closely at Ubuntu, arguably the most popular Linux distribution in the world. It also looks quickly at two other popular distributions, Zorin OS and Linux Mint. This will help illustrate how Linux distributions can differ from one another.

Tip   Do you have an older (but perfectly good) Windows XP laptop or desktop computer you haven't used since Microsoft ceased offering support for the XP platform? Bring it back to life by trying out one of the lightweight Linux distributions; you might be able to delay the need to purchase a new computer for a long while.

Ubuntu: Powering Millions of Laptops and Desktop Computers Around the World

This is the claim made on Ubuntu's website. Ubuntu has become one of the most popular Linux distribution over the past several years. First released in 2004, Ubuntu (the long-term support version is currently 22.04) is designed to be a user-friendly, general-purpose operating system. Ubuntu is a derivative of Debian, a popular Linux distribution backed by a strong community.

Ease of Use

Ubuntu's ease of use adds to its popularity throughout the world.

Ubuntu Desktop

Ubuntu's interface is designed to be easy and intuitive to use. Figure 10-8 shows Ubuntu's default desktop of version 22.04; this release is known as "Jammy Jellyfish."

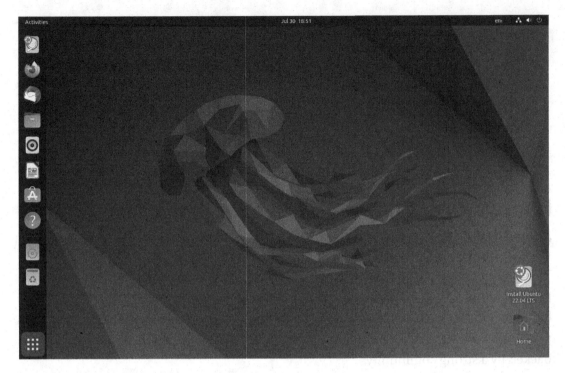

Figure 10-8. *The Ubuntu 22.04 desktop*

The icons of commonly used applications are stored on the left side of the window. Clicking the *Show Applications* (at the very bottom) shows all of the installed applications (Figure 10-9).

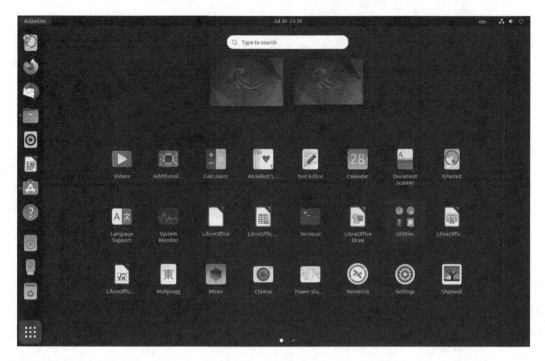

Figure 10-9. *Clicking Show Applications displays the programs installed on Ubuntu*

The desktop environment differs somewhat from that of Windows or Macintosh. As mentioned, the program launch icons are docked on the left side of the screen. Even though this might seem a bit unfamiliar at first for those new to Ubuntu, you will likely grow accustomed to it.

There are a number of wallpapers available to customize the appearance to your liking.

Downloading and Installing Ubuntu Desktop

The current version of Ubuntu Desktop (Figure 10-10) is free to download from the official website's download (`https://ubuntu.com/#download`). Ubuntu is designed to operate under low system requirements to accommodate a wide range of hardware; the system requirements can be viewed here: `https://ubuntu.com/core/docs/system-requirements`.

Figure 10-10. *Ubuntu Desktop can be downloaded at no cost from the official website*

After downloading Ubuntu, it will be necessary to create a bootable USB stick. There are specific instructions on the Ubuntu website on how to accomplish this.

Note   Ubuntu can be tried out by running it from a USB drive without making changes to your computer. Also, if you're not quite ready to give up using Windows (or Mac), Ubuntu can be installed alongside your current operating system, resulting in a dual boot system.

Ubuntu Software

While Microsoft Windows is still by far the dominant force in the computing industry, there are millions of people (as well as businesses and city governments throughout Europe) who have embraced Ubuntu as a viable alternative to Windows. Ubuntu comes preloaded with lots of useful software. There are hundreds of other software titles available for installation on Ubuntu.

One of the most significant programs that comes preinstalled in Ubuntu is *LibreOffice*, the open source office productivity suite (Figure 10-11). LibreOffice is discussed in detail in Chapter 1 of this book.

Figure 10-11. *The powerful LibreOffice is one of the software programs preinstalled in Ubuntu*

Ubuntu also comes with software to view and manage photos, video, and audio. *Shotwell* acquires images from digital cameras and keeps them organized. *Cheese* is an application for taking photos and videos with your webcam. *Rhythmbox* is a music management and playback program (Figure 10-12).

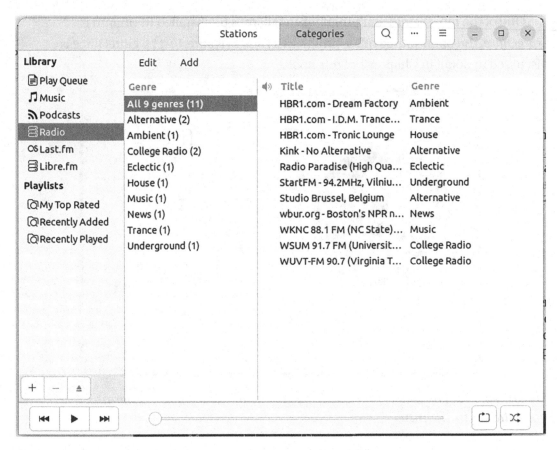

Figure 10-12. *Rhythmbox is a music management and playback program*

There are many other software titles available. By clicking the *Ubuntu Software* icon (shaped like a shopping bag), the software catalog can be accessed. For example, if you need an image editing program such as GIMP, it can be acquired from the Software Center (Figure 10-13). Just press *Install* and the program will be installed on your system in short order.

Figure 10-13. *Acquiring and installing software on Ubuntu is an easy process*

Other useful software programs that can be found in the software catalog are Inkscape (for vector drawing), Kdenlive (for editing video), Krita (a digital drawing and painting program), and many others. There are also a variety of games available for download.

Note   Not all of the software programs available in the Software Center are free, but the majority of them are.

Running Windows Applications on WINE

Despite all of the software available for Ubuntu, some users may still be locked into using a particular Windows program. Yet another perk for Ubuntu and other Linux distributions is the ability to run many legacy Windows software programs on

Linux using a compatibility layer program called WINE. WINE actually stands for Wine Is Not an Emulator, and it is free, open source software that has been around since 1993.

WINE won't support all Windows programs, so it's not a perfect solution. It is an ever evolving project, so in many cases in which a particular Windows program is a must, it might just fill the bill. The WINE website provides information about compatibility.

For more information, visit the WINE website: `www.winehq.org/`.

Security

Ubuntu, like other Linux distributions, is very secure. Anyone who has used Windows for any length of time is aware of the many threats that abound: viruses, malware, worms, Trojan horses, etc. Virus removal is a very high-demand service offered by many computer repair shops. Even the macOS is more open to attack these days.

Although no system is 100% invulnerable, viruses targeting Linux distros are quite rare. More information is available on the Ubuntu Documentation page:

`https://help.ubuntu.com/stable/ubuntu-help/net-antivirus.html.en`

Accessory Compatibility

Ubuntu 22.04 is highly compatible with most devices, such as routers, printers, wireless Wi-Fi adapters, and cameras. The list goes on. If it has a USB connection, Ubuntu will most likely detect it (Figure 10-14).

Figure 10-14. *Ubuntu is compatible with most accessories and devices*

Ubuntu Support

Ubuntu is an easy-to-use operating system. If you are proficient using Windows or Mac, using Ubuntu will be somewhat different at first, but most people can come to grips with it quickly. There are plenty of avenues to explore for support when it's needed. Ubuntu has a strong user base and a very helpful community. The Ask Ubuntu section of the website (https://askubuntu.com/) is a great starting point (Figure 10-15). YouTube hosts a plethora of introductory and instructional videos covering Ubuntu.

Figure 10-15. *The Ask Ubuntu section of the website offers a great deal of support*

Zorin OS: Especially for Newcomers to Linux

Zorin OS (now in version 16.1) is another Linux distribution worth investigating. It's primarily designed for newcomers to Linux, especially those accustomed to working in a Windows environment. Zorin OS is based on Ubuntu, but it has its own developers, support, and community. The official Zorin OS website is http://zorin-os.com/index.html .

Zorin OS comes in several versions: four of them are free and two are paid premium versions. All versions have WINE preinstalled to run many legacy Windows applications.

- **Zorin OS 16.1 Pro (64-bit):** This is a paid version ($39.00) that contains a wide range of software preinstalled. Designed for professional use on modern computers. It can also be configured to resemble other operating systems, such as Windows, macOS, and GNOME. Tech support is available for the paid version of Zorin. There is also a Zorin OS 16.1 Pro Lite for older computers.

- **Zorin OS 16.1 Core (64-bit):** This is a free version of Zorin that contains the core features. It's designed for basic use on modern computers (additional software can be installed when needed).

- **Zorin OS Lite 16.1 (64-bit):** This free version is designed for older, lower spec computers (manufactured as far back as 2007). It provides the essentials needed for web browsing, creating documents, viewing and editing photos, and other functions without the heavier applications.

- **Zorin OS 16.1 Educational (64-bit):** This version is specifically for educational use. There is also a Lite version for older computers.

All of the Zorin 16.1 OS editions receive regular software updates and security updates. Technical support is offered for the paid editions of Zorin OS.

Downloading and Installing Zorin OS

The Zorin OS of your choice (Figure 10-16) can be downloaded from the download page: `https://zorin.com/os/download/`.

The premium version(s) must be purchased before they can be downloaded. Once downloaded, it must be flashed to a USB drive.

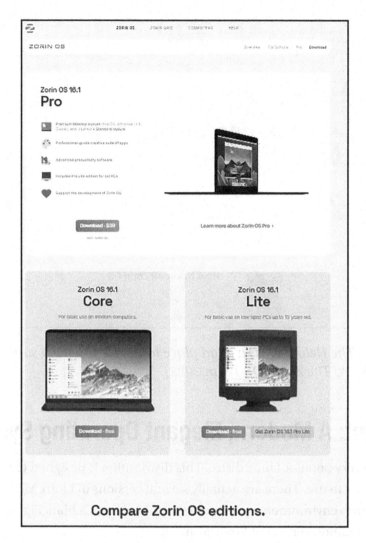

Figure 10-16. *The downloads page for the f Zorin OS edition of your choice (Used with permission © The Zorin OS Team 2022)*

Zorin OS Support

A good place to start if you need support is the *Help* page: https://help.zorin.com/. From here, you'll have access to guides and tutorials (Figure 10-17). There are also numerous YouTube videos to help you with Zorin OS.

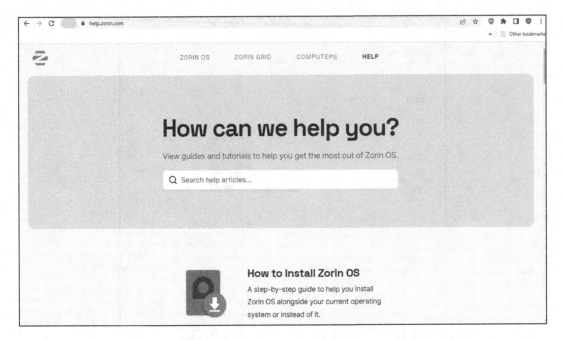

Figure 10-17. *The Help page is a good place to start if you need support. (Used with permission © The Zorin OS Team 2022)*

Linux Mint: A Modern, Elegant Operating System

Linux Mint is a very popular Linux distro. This distribution is designed to be clean, modern, and easy to use. There are actually several versions of Linux Mint, each sporting a different desktop environment based on either Ubuntu or Debian. Figure 10-18 displays the Cinnamon version of Linux Mint 21.

Figure 10-18. *The Linux Mint desktop has a clean, sleek look*

Linux Mint is aimed primarily at home users, but it can be used in a business environment. Like Ubuntu and Zorin OS, there are frequent security and software updates. Applications are launched from the pop-up Menu button (Figure 10-19) on the task bar located on the lower left corner of the screen.

Figure 10-19. *Applications are launched from the Menu*

Note   Part of Linux Mint's appeal is the resemblance of the application launch menu to the Start menu used on Windows. Like Zorin OS, this helps provide a familiar environment for Linux newcomers.

Like other Linux distributions, Mint comes preloaded with software packages for viewing photos, creating documents, etc. Additional software can be acquired from Mint's software repositories by launching the *Software Manager* (Figure 10-20). The menu displays a list of software categories to help you narrow down your search. Using the keyword search feature will pull up a list of the applications that best match your request.

Figure 10-20. *Additional software applications are available from the Software Manager*

Downloading and Installing Linux Mint

The Linux Mint ISO installer can be downloaded from the official website's download page:

    https://linuxmint.com/download.php

There are several versions to choose from, such as the *Cinnamon Edition* (the most popular version), the *MATE Edition* (has fewer features than Cinnamon but runs faster and uses fewer system resources), and the *Xfce Edition* (supports the fewest features, but very stable and light on system resource usage). Just click the *Installation Instructions* button on the download page (Figure 10-21) to access the *Linux Mint Installation Guide*.

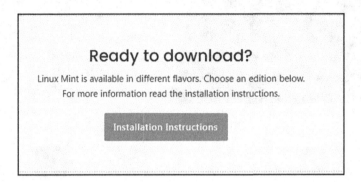

Figure 10-21. *This button takes you to the Linux Mint Installation Guide*

Linux Mint Support

The Documentation page (`https://linuxmint.com/documentation.php`) provides help by providing links to the *Installation Guide*, the *User Guide*, the *Troubleshooting Guide*, the *Translation Guide*, and the *Developer Guide*.

Because Linux Mint is so popular, there's an abundance of help available; click the *Links* tab on the home page to access the forum, blog, and other avenues of information. YouTube hosts plenty of videos pertaining to Linux Mint, including overviews, comparisons of the different versions, and instructional tutorials.

Summary

In this chapter, you learned about the Linux kernel and the various Linux distributions that abound. You learned a little about the origins of Linux and its progression from a system requiring the skills of a computer programmer to the easy-to-use distributions available today.

Linux offers several notable advantages; it's free to download (in most cases), it can be tried out before installing, it comes preloaded with lots of software—the list goes on.

You looked at three distributions: Ubuntu, Zorin OS, and Linux Mint. While they are all the same on a core level, each distribution has unique features built into it. Ubuntu is a very popular distribution around the world, with device compatibility being one of its strongest points. Zorin OS is designed to help transition newcomers accustomed to working in the Windows environment into a Linux environment. Linux Mint is a popular distribution with a clean, modern look.

For those who embrace using a Linux distribution as their OS of choice, it's worth considering giving back to the Linux community in some way, from financial donations to lending expertise on help forums.

APPENDIX A

Professional Profile

Pat David (Figure A-1) is a talented photographer as well as a free and open source software advocate. He can do incredible things with photographic images using the *GNU Image Manipulation Program* (or GIMP), G'MIC (a plug-in utility containing a wide variety of filter effects for GIMP), and other open source photography software.

Figure A-1. *Pat David creates incredible photographic images using open source software. (Used with permission © Patrick David 2015)*

Pat is very active in his advocacy for GIMP. When asked about the advantages of working with free and open source software, his response was this: "The main advantage of F/OSS to me is the community and communication directly with the developers of the tools I use. I've been able to build friendships with the project developers and have been lucky enough to get some ideas integrated into the software. Everyone has been fantastic in the communities to learn from and it's very rewarding to help others realize what they can accomplish using free software!"

Pat runs an open source photography site called PIXLS.US (`https://pixls.us/`). There is a Blog section that highlights upcoming ideas for articles, what's happening in the world of photography, and similar topics. The Articles section (Figure A-2) is an excellent source of "how to" information on image editing using GIMP and other open source software programs. The Discuss section is a forum to connect with others in the open source photography community.

245

© Phillip Whitt 2022
P. Whitt, *Pro Freeware and Open Source Solutions for Business*, https://doi.org/10.1007/978-1-4842-8841-2

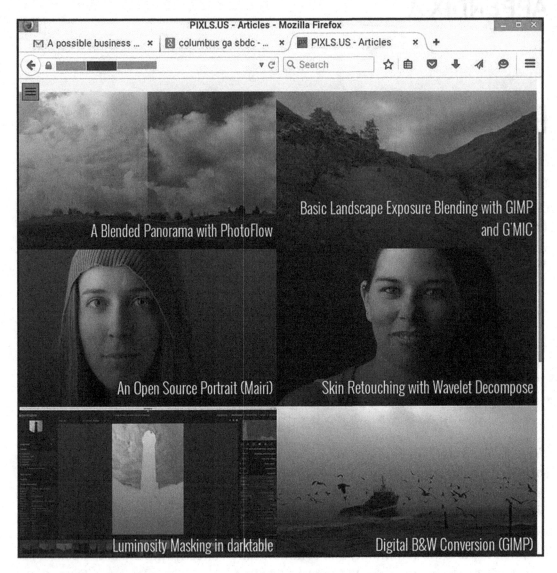

Figure A-2. *PIXLS.US is a great learning resource for open source photography techniques. (Used with permission © Patrick David 2015)*

Additional Software Products

It's certainly my hope that you found useful software solutions in the main portion of this book. However, as I conducted my research for this book, I discovered several additional free software titles. This appendix covers a supplemental list of free software solutions that you may find useful.

Office Productivity, Note Taking, Accounting, and PDF Creation

Here are several software products related to office work similar to the ones in Chapter 1.

Jarte Plus

- **Software description (as shown on the provider's website)**: A free word processor based on the Microsoft WordPad word processing engine built into Windows. A fast-starting, easy-to-use word processor that expands well beyond the WordPad feature set. A small, portable, touch-enabled word processor whose documents are fully compatible with Word and WordPad. (There are paid versions of Jarte available that offer more features.)

- **Website**: www.jarte.com/features.html

- **License**: Proprietary Freeware

- **Current Version**: 6.2

- **Operating System(s)**: Windows

© Phillip Whitt 2022
P. Whitt, *Pro Freeware and Open Source Solutions for Business*, https://doi.org/10.1007/978-1-4842-8841-2

NeoOffice

- **Software description (as shown on the provider's website):**
  NeoOffice is a complete office suite for macOS X. With NeoOffice,
  users can view, edit, and save OpenOffice documents, LibreOffice
  documents, and simple Microsoft Word, Excel, and PowerPoint
  documents. NeoOffice now has a native dark theme.

- **Website:** `www.neooffice.org/neojava/en/index.php`

- **License:** GPL

- **Current Version:** 2022.1 (Professional Edition)

- **Operating System(s):** macOS

KeepNote

- **Software description (as shown on the provider's website):**
  KeepNote is a note-taking application that works on Windows, Linux,
  and macOS X. With KeepNote, you can store your class notes, to-do
  lists, research notes, journal entries, paper outlines, etc. in a simple
  notebook hierarchy with rich-text formatting, images, and more.
  Using full-text search, you can retrieve any note for later reference.

- **Website:** `http://keepnote.org/`

- **License:** GPL

- **Current Version:** 0.7.8

- **Operating System(s):** Windows, macOS, Linux

RedNotebook

- **Software description (as shown on the provider's website):**
  RedNotebook is a modern journal. It includes calendar navigation,
  customizable templates, export functionality, and word clouds. You
  can also format, tag, and search your entries. RedNotebook is free
  software under the GPL.

- **Website**: http://rednotebook.sourceforge.net/index.html
- **License**: GPL
- **Current Version**: 2.25
- **Operating System(s)**: Windows, macOS, Linux

Zoho Books

- **Software description:** Zoho Books offers a free accounting web-based plan for businesses with a revenue less than $50,000 annually. The free plan is for one user + one accountant. It integrates with other Zoho applications.
- **Website:** www.zoho.com/us/books/pricing/
- **License:** Cloud-based free service

Buddi

- **Software provider's description**: "Buddi is a personal finance and budgeting program, aimed at those who have little or no financial background. In making this software, I have attempted to make things as simple as possible, while still retaining enough functions to satisfy most home users."
- **Website**: http://buddi.digitalcave.ca/
- **License**: GPL
- **Current Version**: 3.4.1.16
- **Operating System(s)**: Windows, macOS, Linux

FreePDF

- **Software provider's description:** "The free PDF editor for home or business. Create, edit, view, print, and annotate PDF files... for free!" This is a free Windows-based program that's free to install on up to three computers per family for personal use or one computer for commercial use. This product is by SoftMaker (the maker of FreeOffice). You'll be required to register before downloading.

- **Website:** https://getfreepdf.com/en/

- **License:** Proprietary Freeware

- **Current Version:** 2.1.0

- **Operating System(s):** Windows

PDF Slicer

- **Software provider's description:** "A simple application to extract, merge, rotate, and reorder pages of PDF documents."

- **Website:** https://junrrein.github.io/pdfslicer/

- **License:** GPL

- **Current Version:** 1.8.8

- **Operating System(s):** Windows, Linux

Point-of-Sale, CRM, Backup, and Compression Software

Here are several software products similar to the ones described in Chapter 2.

Regit Express Point-of-Sale for Windows

- **Software provider's description**: "American Precision Instruments has been providing merchants all over the world with powerful, proven, and affordable POS software since we first released Regit POS in 1984. Now American Precision Instrument has released Regit Express, a free, powerful point-of-sale system with a wide range of features that will meet the needs of many retail merchants."

- **Website**: www.free-pos-software.com/

- **License**: Proprietary Freeware

- **Current Version**: 4.0.6.1

- **Operating System(s)**: Windows (the .NET Framework 4.0 or above must be installed, freely available from Microsoft)

monday.com

- **Description**: monday.com is a web-based CRM solution that offers a free individual plan that allows two team members.

- **Website**: https://monday.com

- **License**: Proprietary web-based freeware

- **Current Version**: Unspecified

- **Operating System(s)**: Windows, macOS, Linux

Areca Backup

- **Software provider's description**: It basically allows you to select a set of files/directories to back up, choose where and how (as a simple file copy, as a zip archive, etc.) they will be stored, and configure post-backup actions (like sending backup reports by email or launching custom shell scripts).

- **Website**: www.areca-backup.org/

- **License**: GPL V2

- **Current Version**: 7.5

- **Operating System(s)**: Windows, Linux

PeaZip

- **Software provider's description**: PeaZip is freeware file archiver software, providing a wide array of file management tools, and it is released under Open Source license LGPLv3, which means this application is free of charge for any use (personal and professional, business and government, etc.), modification, and distribution.

- **Website**: `https://peazip.github.io/`

- **License**: LGPL V3

- **Current Version**: 8.7.4

- **Operating System(s)**: Windows, Linux

Illustration, Painting, 3D Modeling Software, and Photo Editing

Here are several software products similar to the ones described in Chapters 3 and 4.

MyPaint

- **Software provider's description**: "MyPaint is a nimble, distraction-free, and easy tool for digital painters. It supports graphics tablets made by Wacom, and many similar devices. Its brush engine is versatile and configurable, and it provides useful, productive tools."

- **Website**: `http://mypaint.org/`

- **License**: GPL 2 (or greater)

- **Current Version**: 2.0.1

- **Operating System(s)**: Windows, macOS, Linux

Sumopaint X

- **Software description**: Sumopaint offers a free, online version that offers basic features and limited storage.
- **Website**: www.sumopaint.com/home/
- **License**: Proprietary Freeware
- **Current Version**: 10.1.5
- **Operating System(s)**: Browser-based

K-3D

- **Software provider's description**: "K-3D is free-as-in-freedom 3D modeling and animation software. It combines flexible plug-ins with a visualization pipeline architecture, making K-3D a versatile and powerful tool for artists."
- **Website**: http://www.k-3d.org/
- **License**: GPL
- **Current Version**:0. 8.0.1
- **Operating System(s)**: Windows, macOS

Photo POS

- **Software provider's description**: "Photo Pos Pro – Complete photo editing suite support everything you'll need to enhance photos and create stunning artworks."
- **Website**: www.free-photo-editor.net/
- **License**: Proprietary Freeware

- **Current Version**: 4
- **Operating System(s)**: Windows

Audio-Video Software

Here are a couple of software products similar to some of the ones seen in Chapter 5.

Audiograbber

- **Software provider's description**: "Audiograbber is a beautiful piece of software that grabs digital audio from CDs. Audiograbber can automatically normalize the music, delete silence from the start and/or end of tracks, and encode them to a variety of formats including MP3. Audiograbber can download and upload disc info from freedb, an Internet compact disc database. You can even record your vinyl LPs or cassette tapes with Audiograbber and make WAVs or MP3s of them. There are a lot more functions in Audiograbber, but to put it simply: Audiograbber has the most features one can wish from such a program!"

- **Website**: www.audiograbber.org/

- **License**: Proprietary Freeware

- **Current Version**: 1.83

- **Operating System(s)**: Windows

Avidemux

- **Software provider's description**: "Avidemux is a free video editor designed for simple cutting, filtering, and encoding tasks. It supports many file types, including AVI, DVD compatible MPEG files, MP4, and ASF, using a variety of codecs. Tasks can be automated using projects, job queues, and powerful scripting capabilities."

- **Website:** http://fixounet.free.fr/avidemux/

- **License:** GPL

- **Current Version:** 2.8

- **Operating System(s):** Windows, macOS, Linux

Brasero

- **Software provider's description:** "Brasero is a GNOME application to burn CD/DVD, designed to be as simple as possible. It has some unique features to enable users to create their discs easily and quickly."

- **Website:** https://wiki.gnome.org/Apps/Brasero

- **License:** GPL

- **Current Version:** 3.12.3-1

- **Operating System(s):** Linux/Unix-like operating systems

Project Management

We looked at ProjectLibre, an open source project management solution listed in Chapter 6, but for good measure here's one more.

Redmine

- **Software provider's description:** "Redmine is a flexible project management web application. Written using the Ruby on Rails framework, it is cross-platform and cross-database. Redmine is open source and released under the terms of the GNU General Public License v2 (GPL)."

- **Website:** www.redmine.org/

- **License**: GPL

- **Current Version**: 5.0.2

- **Operating System(s)**: Redmine should run on most Unix, Linux, Mac, Mac Server, and Windows systems as long as Ruby is available on the platform.

Index

A

Adobe Photoshop, 91, 92, 99, 107, 113

Always Better Control (ABC) Inventory, 178
    add new items, 172, 173
    Almyta Systems, 170
    features, 171, 172
    master list, 173, 174
    New Company Type option window, 172
    support, 174
    tutorial, navigating menus, 174, 175

Antivirus protection
    Avira (*see* Avira)
    ClamAV (*see* ClamAV)

Asana, 178
    features, 166
    home page, 167
    My Tasks page, 167
    new projects, 167
    support, 167
    sync multiple devices, 166
    web-based project management
        tool, 166

Audacity, 127
    click tracks, 137
    digitize radio spots, 134
    easy-to-use multitrack editor, 133
    editing capabilities, 135–137
    features, 133, 134
    installation, 133
    music production, 134
    open source program, editing audio
        files, 132

    record button, 135
    registered trademark, 133, 138
    support, 138
    user manual, 138

AVG Secure Browser, 189
    AVG antivirus software, 184
    features, 186, 187
    Internet, 184
    license, installation on computer, 185
    privacy and security, 185, 186
    Settings menu, 185
    support, 187
    Windows 7, 184

Avira
    features, 212
    free version, 211, 212
    IT security, 211
    support, 212

B

Base, 8, 9

Bitrix24, 60
    collaboration by default, 52
    features, 51
    find, 53, 54
    multiple computers and devices, 50
    multipurpose platform, 50
    profile page, 52, 53
    register, 52
    small business enterprises
        collaboration, 50, 51

© Phillip Whitt 2022
P. Whitt, *Pro Freeware and Open Source Solutions for Business*, https://doi.org/10.1007/978-1-4842-8841-2

F

G

Printed in the United States
by Baker & Taylor Publisher Services